411036

6

Crochet

Dedication
I would like to dedicate this book to my mother, now in her
nineties, who taught me the basic principles of life – including
crochet!   *Wynne Broughton*

An Illustrated
Teach Yourself book

edited and
designed by
Truda Temkin

This beautiful tablecloth could become a family treasure. Make it from individual motifs joined with a simple filling – instructions are given on page 68.

Wynne Broughton

Illustrated Teach Yourself **Crochet**

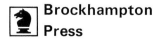
Brockhampton Press

ISBN 0 340 16308 9
First published 1973

746

Published by Brockhampton Press Ltd, Salisbury Road, Leicester
Printed in Great Britain by Fletcher & Son Ltd, Norwich
Text and illustrations copyright © 1973 Brockhampton Press Ltd

Instructions for making all crochet garments, the two
bears, and their illustrations, by courtesy of Lister & Co.
(Knitting Wools Ltd), Wakefield; H. G. Twilley Ltd,
Stamford, and their designer Barbara Warner; Jean
Morton, producer, ATV's programme *Women Today*

Cover photograph, the twisted cord on page 59, and all
crochet photographs in the text, by Herbert Nolan

'Winne' teaching aid photographs, pages 22–6, by T. P. Bartlett

Photograph of hook box, page 9, by courtesy of H. G. Twilley Ltd

Photograph of hooks, page 10, and details of hook sizes,
by courtesy of Abel Morrall Ltd, Redditch

Line drawings by Geoffrey Greiggs. 'Winne' teaching aid designed
by the author. Reproduced by permission of J. W. Spear & Sons
Ltd, Enfield

Contents

Instructions for making these decorative additions to your bedroom are given on page 69.

Introduction

Crochet, that exquisite handicraft with the lacy, intricate look, relies for its beauty on five basic stitches.

The frustration caused by these five stitches to the un-initiated is often difficult for the experienced crocheter to understand, or for the teacher to alleviate. In fact, this early difficulty may well have contributed to the near-demise of crochet during the last half-century.

In the first stages of learning, unsuccessful efforts to work a simple crochet stitch into an uneven, wriggly piece of foundation chain all too frequently cause the beginner to abandon crochet for ever, but once the correct 'hold' has been mastered, the main difficulty has been overcome, and everything else follows easily.

The traditional method of learning is here given in detail, but another, more modern, method is introduced in this book. This is the 'Winne' method, in which the use of a comb-like teaching aid simplifies learning and ensures thorough practice of the basic stitches before working into a foundation chain, making this seemingly awkward man-oeuvre a surprisingly simple operation.

Today there is no limit to the variety of articles awaiting the skill of the crocheter. Almost anything can be produced quite quickly by following a pattern or a chart, or from the worker's own designs. A comprehensive selection of things to make – fashion wear, household articles, toys and accessories – is given later in the book.

Crochet, which no machine can faithfully copy, ranks high in popularity among other handicrafts. It can be worked with equal facility by either the right- or left-handed, and its therapeutic value in certain nervous, rheum-atic and other complaints is recognized by many members of the medical profession.

ITY Crochet is designed to help the beginner, at whatever age, but it is also hoped that it will interest the experienced crocheter who wishes to keep up-to-date with this versatile and fascinating craft in its modern setting.

Note: The 'Winne' beginner's aid is shown on page 11; full instruc-tions for its use are on page 21.
The numbers in brackets in the text refer to the numbered diagrams.

Equipment

Every crocheter should have the best possible equipment and materials for the actual work and, of equal importance, for making up and finishing.

Below is a list of necessities which will lead to efficiency in every stage of the handicraft.

For storage WORK-STAND : a spacious work-stand, with side pockets for various items of equipment, is recommended for keeping everything together. It should be easily washable.

For crochet HOOKS marked in 'international' sizes (see page 10), standard or Tunisian, should be used. Older-style hooks are frequently without size-markings.

HAIRPINS, sometimes known as forks or prongs, are made in various widths (see page 11).

The 'Winne' This useful teaching aid is shown on page 11, and full instructions for its use are given on pages 21–6.

Yarns Good quality yarn should always be used.

For measuring TAPE-MEASURE : a non-stretch type gives greater accuracy.

RULER : a 12 in. (30 cms) transparent ruler is useful. An 8 in. measure (20 cms) is shown on this page.

For cutting SCISSORS : keep a sharp pair of scissors handy; many modern yarns cannot be broken off by hand.

For sewing up NEEDLES : large-eyed, blunt-ended wool types will be needed for the thicker yarns, and similar kinds in smaller sizes for finer yarns and cottons. Ordinary sewing needles will be required for sewing on buttons, press studs, hooks and eyes, etc. Keep all needles together in a suitable container.

BODKINS in several sizes are useful for threading elastic, belts and other work, and should be kept with the needles.

PINS : a good supply of dressmaker's steel pins, which will not mark the work, should be kept in a separate container. Small safety pins make useful markers on the work.

THIMBLE : a well-fitting thimble makes sewing more comfortable.

For pressing A STEAM-IRON eliminates the need for a damp cloth. An ordinary heat-controlled iron is also suitable.

IRONING BOARD : this should always have a spotlessly clean cover and should be well padded.

PRESSING CLOTH : a piece of fine cotton or muslin measuring about ¾ yd (68·6 cms) square will make a suitable cloth.

SLEEVE BOARD : a useful optional extra for pressing short sleeves and seams. A good substitute is a pad of cotton material folded to 1 in. (2½ cms) thick, and 4 in. (10 cms) longer than the longest seam to be pressed, and at least 2 in. (5 cms) wider than the iron.

Some extra items A ROW COUNTER saves time and avoids defacing patterns with written notes.

A HOOK BOX, like the two-compartment box illustrated here, will keep all hooks together, as well as providing a place for the Winne, a pencil and the row counter.

A useful hook box

Hooks and Hairpins

Crochet hooks   Hooks fall into three main categories:

1. The larger sizes which are used mainly for wools and similar yarns, and for the thicker cottons.
2. The smaller sizes are designed for use with finer cotton and silk threads.
3. Tunisian (also known as Tricot or Afghan) hooks, which are available in varying lengths.

With the exception of Tunisian hooks, all modern hooks have a flattened section along part of the shank, designed for ease of holding. On this the hook size is marked.

International standard sizes

2	4	5	6	7	8	9
7.00	6.00	5.50	5.00	4.50	4.00	3.50

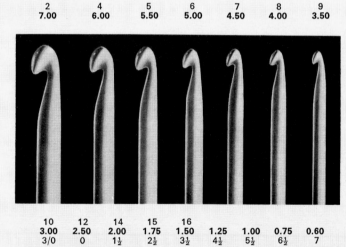

The illustrations show, in actual size, the international standard range of hook sizes, adopted by agreement, and in use since July 1969. These sizes are now used in printed crochet patterns. Equivalent old and new hook sizes are given here.

The new international sizes are given in bold. The figures above are the 'old' wool sizes. The figures below are the 'old' cotton sizes.

10	12	14	15	16				
3.00	2.50	2.00	1.75	1.50	1.25	1.00	0.75	0.60
3/0	0	1½	2½	3½	4½	5½	6½	7

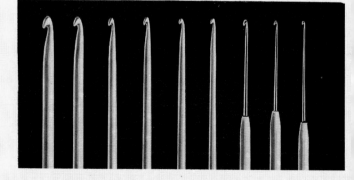

Tunisian hooks

These hooks follow the international range of sizes, and are made in various lengths according to the width of work to be done. Each hook has a stitch-retaining knob at the end.

Hairpin, prong or fork

Hairpin crochet is a specialized form of the handicraft, for which both the hairpin implement and a hook are used.

Hairpins, measured by width, are made in sizes ½ in., ¾ in., 1 in., 1¼ in., 1½ in., 1¾ in., 2 in., 2½ in. and 3 in.

The 'Winne' teaching aid

This new modern aid to crochet-learning is a comb-like holder, made in one size, measuring 8 in. (20 cms) wide. It has 20 teeth, each with a round hole through which the yarn is threaded for the first row. Between each tooth is a square opening for hook access.

It is made in stout plastic and may be obtained from J. W. Spear & Sons Ltd, Enfield, Middlesex. Full instructions for using the Winne are given on pages 21–6.

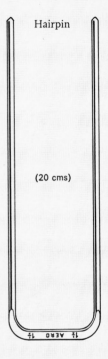

Hairpin

(20 cms)

The Winne teaching aid, about half actual size

Tunisian
hook, about two-thirds
actual size

Yarn

Yarn is the collective term used today for all threads suitable for crochet and other handicrafts, from the thickest of wools to the synthetics, and including cottons and silks.

Modern yarns fall into three main categories:

1. Natural fibres, such as pure wool and cotton
2. Synthetics, or man-made yarns
3. Mixtures of 1 and 2.

One great advantage of pure wool over its synthetic counterparts and cotton is that it will absorb up to 20 per cent of its own weight in water before striking cold to the skin. Through its built-in insulation against sudden changes of temperature, it is particularly safe and snug for children's garments and for general outdoor wear.

Cottons, in many types and thicknesses, have long proved highly successful in crochet work, but today they have assumed a glamour of their own and are well established on the fashion scene.

Most modern yarns are specially treated against the ravages of the moth. Flareproofing and shrink-resistant properties are also added where possible during the processing, without detracting from the quality of the yarn itself.

Metrication All yarn manufacturers have metrication in mind. Until standardization is agreed, most yarns are now marked in ounces and grams, or in yards and metres. The following are equivalents in ounces and grams:

Ounces and grams

1 ounce = 28·35 grams	5 ounces = 141·75 grams
2 ounces = 56·70 grams	10 ounces = 283·50 grams

A guide to working out requirements is given below:

	No. of balls required		
ounces	20 gram balls	25 gram balls	50 gram balls
1	2	2	1
2	3	3	2
5	8	6	3
10	15	12	6

Some advice Always buy at the outset sufficient yarn of the brand recommended in the pattern to complete the article to be made. Stocks may run out and dyes sometimes vary, and you may have difficulty in matching. If you are unable to obtain the yarn specified, the manufacturer will send a list of the nearest stockists on request.

If you are working without a pattern, always buy the best quality yarn you can afford.

When working to larger or smaller measurements than the pattern gives, remember to adjust the quantities accordingly.

Always keep an empty spool, or ball band; it gives the shade number and dye lot number, and is useful for reordering.

Learning to crochet

With the introduction of the 'Winne' method there are two ways of learning the basic stitches of crochet.

1. THE TRADITIONAL METHOD

Crochet generally is worked in two ways:

1. In rows, from right to left. (In the case of the left-handed, from left to right.) The work is turned round at the end of each row in readiness for the beginning of the next.
2. In rounds, for circular or square work. Each round is levelled up at the end with a slip stitch, or other stitch indicated in the pattern.

2. THE 'WINNE' METHOD

This is a new and unique operation which simplifies and speeds up learning. During only a very short period of concentrated practice, all the basic stitches, consistency of stitch formation, motif work and elementary pattern reading can be accomplished without difficulty.

THE TRADITIONAL METHOD

The slip knot start

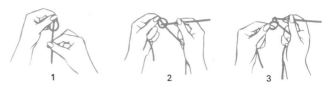

Take yarn in left hand a few inches from the end, and form it into a circle. Drop end down back of circle (1). Holding circle between thumb and 1st finger, take up the hook in right hand, insert it through centre of circle, catching yarn in hook (2). Pull down end, keeping loop on hook (3).

Yarn control holds Either of the two holds illustrated may be used.

Holding knot and hook between thumb and 1st finger of left hand, take yarn from ball over 1st and 2nd fingers, slightly raising 2nd finger, then under 3rd finger, and right round 4th finger (4).

Take yarn from ball round 4th finger of left hand, then through to back of hand between 2nd and 3rd fingers, over slightly raised 2nd finger and 1st. Bend down 4th finger to control yarn (5).

For left-handed workers

Diagrams (6) and (7) illustrate the reversed procedure for holds (4) and (5).

Turning the work   Before proceeding to learn the basic stitches it is necessary
to study the *turning chain*, that is, the number of chain
stitches to be made at the beginning of each row, in order
to bring hook and yarn into the correct position for the row
to come.

The turning chain forms the first stitch of the new row.
No stitch is therefore worked into the top of the last stitch
of the previous row, unless increasing. Printed patterns will
sometimes denote this as 'miss first stitch', that is, d.c., tr.,
or whichever stitch was made at the end of the previous
row.

Directions usually state the number of chains the various
stitches require to turn, as follows:

double crochet:	1 ch. to turn
half treble:	2 ch. to turn
treble:	3 ch. to turn
double treble:	4 ch. to turn
triple treble:	5 ch. to turn
quadruple treble:	6 ch. to turn
quintuple treble:	7 ch. to turn

Exceptions   In the case of double crochet only, some patterns omit
the 1 turning chain in favour of 1 d.c.

In fashion wear, the turning chain for treble is sometimes reduced from 3 to 2, to give a firmer edge. Similarly,
those for double, triple, quadruple and quintuple trebles
are each reduced by 1 ch., to 3, 4, 5 and 6, respectively.

Turning chains   In the instructional drawings, the foundation chain is
and new stitches   shown in outline, the turning chains are shaded, and the
new stitches are indicated by black lines. The accompanying
drawing (8) illustrates this scheme.

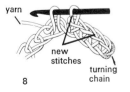

yarn

new
stitches

turning
8   chain

End stitches

In plain patterns, the last stitch at the end of a row is
worked into the turning chain of the previous row. Patterns usually state exactly which chain to enter; this
should always be counted from the bottom. The drawings
which follow show clearly the position of the turning
chain.

The chain (ch.)

Most crochet, whether it is worked backwards and forwards in rows, or round and round in circles, begins with a length of chain. Exceptions to this are *Working in circles, winding start* page 20, and *Borders worked directly on to fabric, necks, sleeves, hems* page 40.

With the loop already on hook as in diagram (3), and the yarn in working position as in (4), (5) or (6), (7) for left-handed hold, *pass yarn over hook (y.o.h.) (9), then pull hook through loop already on hook. 1 ch. stitch made. Repeat from *29 times, to make 30 ch. stitches altogether, a suitable length to work on.

Inspection of the foundation chain will reveal a row of chain stitches with a third connecting thread. When working into the foundation chain this link must be taken up into the hook with the top loop of the chain (10). This connecting link has been omitted to simplify the drawings, but the instructions for each stitch include this rule which, unless a pattern instructs otherwise, should always be followed both when working into a foundation chain and into future chains or stitches of other rows or rounds.

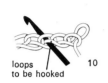

loops to be hooked   10

The first row of slip stitches (s.s.)

Sometimes called *single crochet* (s.c.).

This will be worked into the 30 ch. foundation row already made.

Insert hook into 2 loops of 2nd ch. from hook, y.o.h. and draw through stitch and loop on hook. First s.s. completed.

Insert hook into next ch., y.o.h. and draw through stitch and loop on hook. 2nd s.s. completed (11).

Repeat from * to * to end of foundation ch. 29 s.s. made plus 1 turning ch. = 30 sts.

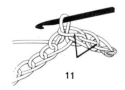

11

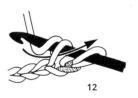

12

13

14

The first row of double crochet (d.c.)

Make 30 ch. as before.

Ignoring the 30th ch. (that is, the turning ch. which will form the first stitch of the row of d.c. now to be made), insert hook into 2 loops of the 29th ch. (2nd ch. from hook), taking yarn over hook (y.o.h.) (12); draw hooked yarn through 2 chain loops just picked up (2 loops on hook), y.o.h. again (13); and draw through both loops on hook. First d.c. made (14).

**Insert hook into 2 loops of next foundation ch. stitch, y.o.h. and draw through ch. just picked up, y.o.h. again and draw through both loops. (15) shows 3 d.c. made, plus 1 turning ch. = 4 stitches.

Repeat from ** making 1 d.c. into every ch. to end of foundation ch. 29 d.c. made plus 1 turning ch. = 30 sts.

15

Practice

Undo the work so far, and begin again from the slip knot, repeating the actions until hook and hands work smoothly together.

The first row of half treble (hlf.tr.)

Make a 30 ch. foundation row.

Y.o.h. (16), insert hook into 2 loops of 28th ch. (3rd ch. from hook), y.o.h. (17), and pull this through ch. loops just picked up (3 loops on hook), y.o.h. again (18), and pull this through all 3 loops on hook (1 loop on hook). First hlf.tr. made.

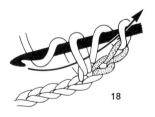

16

17

18

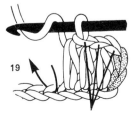

19

Y.o.h., insert hook into 2 loops of next ch. stitch, y.o.h., and pull through ch. stitch just picked up, y.o.h. again, and pull through all 3 loops on hook. 2nd hlf.tr. made. (19) shows 3 hlf.tr. made, plus 2 turning ch. = 4 stitches.

Repeat from *, making 1 hlf.tr. into every ch. to end of foundation ch. 28 hlf.tr. made, plus turning ch. = 29 stitches.

The first row of treble (tr.)

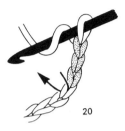

20

Make 30 ch. as before.

Y.o.h. (20), insert hook into 2 loops of 27th ch. (4th ch. from hook), y.o.h. (21), and pull this through ch. stitch just picked up (3 loops on hook), y.o.h. (22), and pull this through first 2 loops on hook (2 loops on hook), y.o.h. again (23), and pull through remaining 2 loops. 1 loop on hook. First tr. completed.

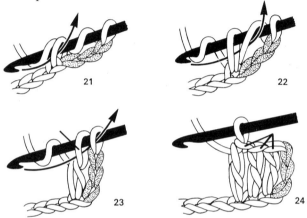

21

22

23

24

Y.o.h., insert hook into 2 loops of next ch., y.o.h. and pull through ch. stitch just picked up, y.o.h. and pull through first 2 loops on hook, y.o.h. and pull through remaining 2 loops. 2nd tr. made. (24) shows 3 tr. made plus 3 turning ch. = 4 stitches. Rep. from * to * to end of foundation ch. 27 tr. made, plus 3 turning ch. = 28 stitches.

The first row of double treble (dbl.tr.)

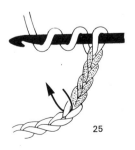

25

Make 30 ch. as before.

Y.o.h. *twice* (25), insert hook into 2 loops of 26th ch. (5th ch. from hook) (26), y.o.h. and pull through ch. stitch just picked up (4 loops on hook), y.o.h. (27) and pull through first 2 loops on hook (3 loops on hook), y.o.h. (28), and pull through next 2 loops, y.o.h. (29), and pull through last 2 loops. 1 loop on hook. First dbl.tr. made.

26

27

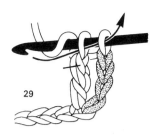

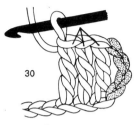

Y.o.h. twice, insert hook into next ch., y.o.h. and pull through ch. stitch just picked up, y.o.h. and pull through first 2 loops on hook, y.o.h. and pull through next 2 loops, y.o.h. and pull through last 2 loops. 2nd dbl.tr. made. (30) shows 3 dbl.tr. made plus 4 turning ch. = 4 stitches.

Repeat from * to * to end of foundation ch. 26 dbl.tr. made plus 4 turning ch. = 27 sts.

The first row of triple treble (trip.tr.)

Make 30 ch. as before. Y.o.h. *three times* (31), insert hook into 2 loops of 25th ch. (6th ch. from hook), y.o.h. (32), and pull through ch. stitch just picked up (5 loops on hook), y.o.h. (33), and pull through first 2 loops on hook (4 loops on hook), y.o.h. (34), and pull through next 2 loops on hook (3 loops on hook), y.o.h. (35), and pull through next 2 loops, y.o.h. (36) and pull through last 2 loops. 1 loop on hook. 1st trip.tr. made.

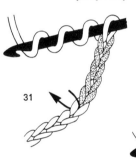

*Y.o.h. three times, insert hook into next ch., y.o.h., and pull through ch. stitch just picked up, y.o.h., and pull through first 2 loops on hook, y.o.h. and pull through next 2 loops, y.o.h. and pull through next 2 loops, y.o.h. and pull through last 2 loops. 2nd trip.tr. made. (37) shows 3 trip.tr. made. Rep. from * to end of foundation ch. 25 trip.tr. made plus 5 turning ch. = 26 sts.

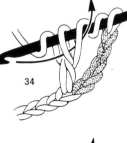

Quadruple and quintuple treble

These stitches are made similarly to double and triple treble, 2 loops being taken off the hook each time the yarn is hooked.

For quadruple treble the yarn is hooked 4 times before entry into the 7th foundation ch. from the hook.

For quintuple treble the yarn is hooked 5 times before entry into the 8th foundation ch. from hook.

Working in circles

38

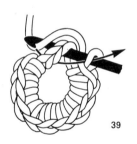

39

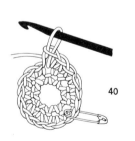

40

Most circular work begins with several chain stitches joined by a slip stitch to form a ring. Alternatives are given below. All patterns explain in detail the stitches which follow.

When working in rounds, the last stitch at the end of one round is joined to the first stitch of that round, to make the stitches level. In plain fabric this is usually done with a slip stitch. To begin the next round, the yarn must be brought to the correct height for the next stitch to be made.

When working in double crochet, the first stitch of the new round may be made either by 1 d.c. or by 1 ch.; for hlf.tr. by 2 ch.; for tr. by 3 ch.; for dbl.tr. by 4 ch.; and so on.

The following simple exercise gives the basic principle of working in rounds.

To begin: Make 7 ch., join into a ring with 1 s.s. into first ch. (38).

1st round: *Make 1 d.c. by passing hook through centre of ring (39), y.o.h. and pull hook back through ring (2 loops on hook), y.o.h. again, and pull through both loops. First d.c. made. Rep. from * 13 times. 14 d.c. made. Join with 1 s.s. to first st. of round. Mark end of this round with a small safety pin, or piece of contrast yarn (40).

2nd round: 1 ch. (or 1 d.c.), (2 d.c. in next st., 1 d.c. in next st.) 6 times, 2 d.c. in last st., join with 1 s.s. to first st. of round.

Note : to keep the work flat, gradual increases are necessary as the circle grows in circumference. Patterns always clearly denote these.

Alternatives to chain starting-ring

The winding start

Wind yarn several times round finger, or any object of the required circumference. Remove ring so formed.

For starting loop, insert hook into ring, y.o.h. and pull

Winding start. 6 strands followed by double crochet stitches.

hook back through ring; y.o.h. and pull through loop on hook. Proceed as for first round of chain-ring start, working the first round over the loose end of yarn.

If a thicker texture is required for the continuing work, 2 or more strands of the yarn, or a length of piping cord, may be worked over as desired.

The curtain-ring start

A curtain-ring may be worked over as in the winding start.

For starting loop, insert hook into ring, loop yarn over hook, and pull back through ring, double y.o.h. and pull through loop on hook. Release short end (to be sewn in neatly afterwards). Follow by double crochet or treble stitches until the ring is covered.

If the design requires rings to be joined, the first completed ring can be joined to the one in work by a slip stitch, or the rings may be sewn together later.

Curtain rings covered in double crochet stitches, joined with a slip stitch.

THE 'WINNE' METHOD

To learn to use the Winne the beginner will need: the crochet teaching aid, a crochet hook size 5·00 to 3·50, 1 ball yarn and 1 wool needle.

The 5 basic crochet stitches will be learned in the following order (abbreviations in brackets):

1. Chain (ch.)
2. Double crochet (d.c.)
3. Half treble (hlf.tr.)
4. Treble (tr.)
5. Slip stitch (s.s.), or single crochet (s.c.)

Other abbreviations* :
yarn over hook, or catch yarn with hook (y.o.h.)
stitch(es) (st(s).)

* A comprehensive list of abbreviations in general use for crochet work is given on page 60.

To turn work at end of row: In crochet, chain stitches are added at the end of a row to prepare for the next row. The work is then turned round so that the reverse side is facing the worker. Left-handed learners can easily work according to the instructions, or may reverse them by threading base row yarn from B* to A, starting work at U, and reversing all the lettering. A mirror placed opposite the pictures will assist the action.

In the following instructions the teaching aid will be referred to as 'the Winne'.

Method To form base row, which on the Winne takes the place of the usual length of starting chain stitches, use a wool needle and thread yarn backwards and forwards fairly tightly through round holes A to B. Fix end of yarn at B with a piece of adhesive tape or a knot. Base row completed.

The hold Hold the Winne in left hand under gap C between thumb and first finger. There are various ways of holding the yarn,

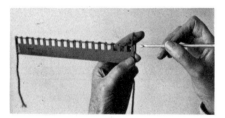

The hold

and the simple one given here may be adapted to individual needs. Alternative holds are shown on p. 12.

Take yarn from A over first 3 fingers of left hand, then under the 4th which should be bent right down over the yarn to control its flow from the ball. Slightly curve and raise 2nd finger about ½ in. above first, for here the yarn will always go over and into the hook (y.o.h.).

Take the hook in other hand, holding it *all the time* between thumb and first finger at flattened part of stem, the hook end always facing the worker. The illustration shows the hold.

* These letters refer to the letters marked on the Winne.

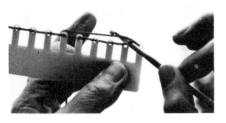

The starting loop

Insert hook from front to back of the Winne *under* base row through gap C, and catch yarn in hook (y.o.h.) below raised 2nd finger.

Draw hook back through C under base row the same way as it went in. Starting loop now on hook.

Chain (ch.)

1 chain stitch will now be made to form the first stitch of the row of double crochets to follow, thus: over top of the Winne catch yarn with hook (y.o.h.) under raised 2nd finger.

Pull the yarn just hooked through loop already on hook. 1 ch. made.

Double crochet (d.c.)

*Insert hook through gap C under base row, catch yarn with hook (y.o.h.), and draw hook back through C (2 loops on hook). The illustration shows hook just returning to front of work. *continued*

Double crochet (d.c.) continued

Now, y.o.h. over top of the Winne, and draw yarn just hooked through the 2 loops on hook (1 loop now on hook).* 1 d.c. made.

Make 2 d.c. in each gap from D to U by repeating the instructions between the two asterisks * to *, substituting in turn the letters D to U for C, and moving thumb and first finger along the Winne under each new stitch being made. 37 d.c. made, plus starting ch. = 38 stitches (sts.).

Practice　*Now undo the whole row*, and repeat from starting loop again and again until easy rhythm of movement is obtained, and an evenly formed row of double crochet stitches appears, in readiness for the row of half trebles (hlf.tr.) to follow. These will be worked into the row of chain stitches which will be seen at the top of the double crochet stitches, and will provide practice in readiness for working stitches into a basic chain later on.

Half treble (hlf.tr.)

Now with 1 row of perfectly formed double crochet stitches on the Winne, make 2 ch. for the turning chain by placing y.o.h. and pulling through loop already on hook, twice. (Turning ch. made.)

Turn the Winne round to begin the new row. Ignoring the st. at base of turning ch. just made, *y.o.h., and insert hook under both loops of next ch. st. at the top of next d.c. of previous row.

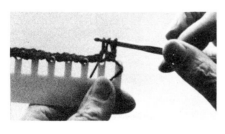

Y.o.h. again, and draw this through new top ch. st. just picked up (3 loops on hook).

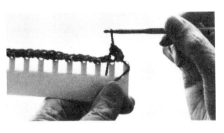

Y.o.h. again, and draw this thread through all loops on hook (1 loop on hook), 1 hlf.tr. made.* Repeat from * to * making 1 hlf.tr. into each top ch. st. of previous row, working the last hlf.tr. into top of starting ch. of previous row. 37 hlf.tr. made plus turning ch. = 38 sts.

Try to cultivate the habit of counting the stitches, always making sure all end stitches are worked into.

Treble (tr.)

Make 3 turning ch., by placing y.o.h. and pulling it through loop on hook, 3 times. Turn the Winne round, ready for the new row of trebles.

Ignoring the st. at base of turning ch. just made, *y.o.h., insert hook into next top ch. st., y.o.h. and pull this thread through st. just picked up (3 loops on hook), y.o.h. again, and pull this through first 2 loops on hook (2 loops on hook), y.o.h. again and pull this through remaining 2 loops on hook (1 loop on hook).* First tr.st. made.

Repeat from * to * making 1 tr. over next and every succeeding hlf.tr. of previous row, the last tr. being made into top of turning ch. of previous row. 37 tr. made plus turning ch. = 38 sts.

Note: Double treble, triple treble, quadruple treble, quintuple treble, are all worked similarly to treble.

Slip stitch (s.s.) sometimes called
Single crochet

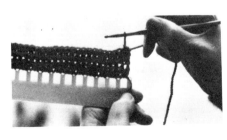

Make no turning ch., turn the Winne round. *Insert hook into first top ch. st. of previous row, y.o.h. and, holding work well down, pull this thread through both loops on hook.* 1 s.s. (or s.c.) made. Repeat from * to * to end of row, making 1 s.s. into each st. of previous row. 38 s.s.

continued

Practice is important

These basic stitches form the foundation of all crochet. Practise them well until tension is even and each individual stitch is easily recognized.

To remove work from the Winne

This may be done at any time after the first two rows of crochet have been worked, or left until the last row is completed.

Release end of yarn at base row B, and unlace it along base row to A. The stitches will not run.

To finish off this first row, insert hook in the loop at the base of first and second 'sts. at opposite end to dangling base row yarn, pull second loop through first, insert hook in third loop and pull this through loop on hook. Continue in this way to end of row. Pull base row yarn end through loop on hook, and fasten off securely.

To fasten off

Break off yarn, draw this through the loop on hook, and pull up tightly. Sew end neatly into work. It will be appreciated that the Winne is an aid to learning the basic technique of crochet; once ease of working has been achieved, a full-size piece of work can be attempted.

The cover

The crochet shown on the cover was designed and worked especially for this book by Carol Outram, D.A.D. Miss Outram did post-graduate teaching at Brighton, and now teaches the craft of contemporary crochet at the Camden Institute in London.

**Sparkling
collar and cuffs**

Adding a pretty collar and cuff set to a plain dress is a wonderful improvement – the set can be worked from the instructions on page 73.

General information

Tension Tension means the number of stitches, or patterns, to a given measurement.

Unfortunately, all too often it is regarded as an unnecessary, boring chore. Yet it is the most important part of all directions. It can never be too strongly emphasized that tension instructions, which are always printed at the beginning of every pattern, should be strictly followed.

Designers take tremendous trouble to ensure that the tension of all patterns is checked again and again before distribution to the public. In crochet, tension can vary so much from person to person that inaccuracy may all too easily develop into a sad, mis-shaped failure.

Always make it a golden rule to *work the tension test first*, using the hook and yarn recommended in the pattern. If the sample is too large, try again with a smaller-sized hook. If too small, try a larger hook. If there is still fractional doubt, work another tension piece at least twice as large as the pattern suggests. Then select the hook which gives the correct measurement.

Beginners should always choose a simple, one-line pattern as the first venture into production. Before deciding, the abbreviations and other preliminary data should be thoroughly understood.

No crocheter should ever embark on anything which is destined to lie idle for long periods between crocheting sessions. This will inevitably lead to variations in tension, with disappointing results.

The tension test has another great advantage, for it familiarizes the crocheter with the particular stitch, or pattern, before the main work begins.

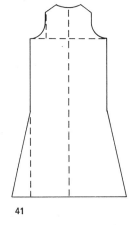

41

Measuring the work

Never measure along the edges of any crochet work. Place the article to be measured on a table, the floor, or any other flat surface, and measure from the centre.

Armholes are always measured on the straight, never along the curve. The accompanying diagrams, (41) and (42), show the correct measuring points.

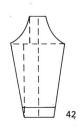

42

Increasing   In plain fabric this is done by working 2 stitches into 1 of the previous row, at the beginning, the end, or during a row or round.

This example shows 1 tr. increase at beginning and end of 2nd and 3rd rows, and 1 tr. increase in alternate stitches of 3rd row.

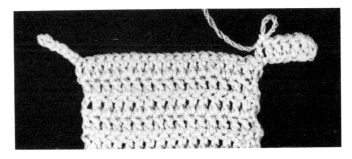

Example shows a 6-stitch increase at beginning and end of row.

Where increasing is required at the beginning and end of a row, this is done by making the required number of chain stitches at the beginning of the row. Using a separate length of yarn, join this to the end of the row, at the same level as the extra chains at the beginning; and make the required number of chains. Work into all the extra chains as in foundation chains.

Decreasing   Some decreases, such as those for neck and armhole, are made at the edges of the work.

This is done by making 1 slip stitch over each stitch to be decreased at the beginning of the row, and leaving unworked the same number at the end of the row, if the decreasings are symmetrical.

The illustration on the next page shows a decrease of 3 stitches at the beginning and end of a row, followed by 1 decrease at each end of the next 2 rows.

Decreasing at row ends

Decreasing during the row

To decrease within the row, it is sometimes possible unobtrusively to miss 1 stitch of the previous row.

Where this cannot be done, to decrease 1 stitch, work 1 stitch at the appropriate point, leaving the last loop of this stitch on the hook, work the next stitch leaving 1 loop of this stitch on the hook, y.o.h., and take off all loops. There will be 1 chain top stitch to work into in the next row, instead of 2.

Similarly, 2 stitches may be decreased at the same point by leaving unworked the last loop of 3 stitches, y.o.h. and take off all loops. There will be 1 chain top stitch to work into in the next row, instead of 3.

The example shows, in the 3rd row, 1 decrease over 2nd and 3rd treble stitches of 2nd row, and 2 decreases over the 5th, 6th and 7th treble stitches of the 2nd row.

Counting the rows

A row counter is useful for recording the number of rows worked. It is also a great time saver when counting pattern rows.

Mistakes

There is only one way to rectify a mistake. Undo the work down to the error, and begin again from there.

Crochet stitches, unlike those in knitting, do not run up or down the fabric as it is undone.

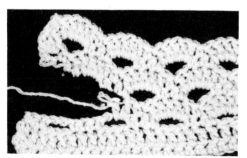

Pulled thread

To shorten a garment

Measure and mark the exact length required.

A length of work may be removed by cutting the thread which connects two rows, at the end of the row, then pulling undone the thread along the row.

The row of loops left at the base of the new first row of the work may be finished off by double crochet stitches, or another suitable edging.

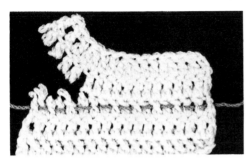

An alternative method is to run a length of contrasting yarn through the row below the marked length required. Cut through all the stitches which connect this row with the one above. Pull out the loose threads, and work into the edge loops as above.

Cut thread

Joining the yarn A good crocheter will never allow a knot to appear anywhere in the work, although a knot made at the end of a row which will be worked invisibly into a seam is permissible. Badly joined yarn will spoil the appearance by causing unevenness of texture.

Where possible, joins should be made at the end of the row, within several inches of the end of the yarn.

There are several ways of making neat joins. The simplest method, which can be used at any point along a row, is to lay the end of the old ball along the top of the next few stitches to be worked. Then loop the new yarn over the hook, and continue working from the new ball, working over both ends for a few stitches to secure them (43).

43

Another way, when joining yarn of the same colour, is to work over the new end for a few stitches still using the old ball, then take up the new ball and continue to work the stitches with this, working several stitches over the yarn from the old ball.

When working in stripes, as for the chevron pattern, illustrated on page 35, 'steps' in colours will be avoided if the last loop of the last stitch of the last row is worked in the new colour.

To join a new colour a little distance from the old, as in the coloured treble-and-chain square, insert hook into the required stitch, loop yarn over hook, and pull through the stitch; work 1 ch. using yarn double, then discard the loose end and continue working from the ball.

Tingha and Tucker – two famous bears

These famous bears will delight the little ones. Designed by the author, they are worked in Lister's Fun-Fur-Knit. Instructions are given on page 88.

Stitch combinations

The really exciting part of crochet begins when patterns formed by stitch combinations are attempted.

The following stitch combinations provide exercises in pattern reading, and give the beginner some idea of the potential of the crocheter who may wish later to adapt a favourite pattern to a chosen style.

In some of the examples a specific number of foundation chain stitches is given. These may be increased as desired.

Working these patterns presents an opportunity to cultivate the habit of recognizing and counting stitches and rows, with plenty of end-stitch practice.

Remember that crochet is worked upwards, so that any reference to the first row of an example in the following instructions means the bottom row on the illustrations.

Bar and lacet

Begin with 32 ch.

BAR ROW 1 : 1 tr. in 14th ch. from hook (this allows 5 ch. for foundation bar, 3 ch. for turn and 5 ch. for top bar), *5 ch., miss 5 ch., 1 tr. in next ch. Rep. from * to end of ch., 6 ch., turn (ready for lacet row).

LACET ROW : 1 d.c. in 3rd (centre) ch. of bar, 3 ch., miss 2 sts., 1 tr. into next tr. (i.e. tr. over tr.) (1 lacet worked), *3 ch., miss 2 sts., 1 d.c. into next st., 3 ch., miss 2 sts., 1 tr. over next tr. (2 lacets made). Rep. from * to end of row, making last tr. into turning ch. of first row. 8 ch., turn (this allows 3 ch. for the turn and 5 ch. for the first bar in next row).

BAR ROW 2 : Miss 1st lacet, 1 tr. into next tr., *5 ch., 1 tr. in next tr. Rep. from * making last tr. into 3rd of 6 turning ch., 6 ch., turn.

Repeat lacet and bar row 2 alternately.

This pattern gives a charming lacy appearance and it could be used in a variety of ways.

Blocks and spaces

Bobbles

Chain lace

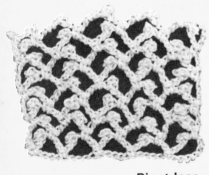

Picot lace

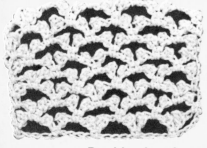

Double picot lace

Blocks and spaces

Begin with 30 ch.

1ST ROW : 1 tr. into 4th ch. from hook, 1 tr. into each of next 2 ch. (first block made), *2 ch., miss 2 ch., 1 tr. into each of next 4 ch. (1 sp. and 1 more block made). Rep. from * to end of ch., 3 ch., turn.

Block over block

2ND ROW : 1 tr. over each of next 3 tr. (first block over block made), *2 ch., miss 2 ch., 1 tr. into each of next 4 sts. (first sp. over sp. and 2nd block made). Rep. from *, making space over space and block over block to end of row.
See first 2 rows of example.

Alternate blocks and spaces

3RD ROW : 5 ch. (this allows 3 ch. for turn and 2 ch. for first sp. over first block), 1 tr. in next st., 2 tr. into space below, 1 tr. in next st. (first block over space worked), *2 ch., miss 2 sts., 1 tr. in next st., 2 tr. in space, 1 tr. in next st. Rep. from *, working last tr. of last sp. into 3rd of 3 turning ch., 3 ch., turn.

4TH ROW : 2 tr. in first sp., 1 tr. in next st., *2 ch., miss 2 sts., 1 tr. over next tr., 2 tr. in space, 1 tr. over next tr. Rep. from *, making alternate block over space to end of row, working last tr. of last block into 3rd of 5 turning ch.
See rows 3 and 4 of example.

Bobbles

These may be worked into a foundation ch. or other stitch. *Y.o.h., insert hook into st., y.o.h. and draw loop up to ½ in., or more, according to height required (y.o.h., insert hook into same st., y.o.h., and draw yarn up to same height) 3 times (4 times in all), y.o.h., and draw through all 9 loops on hook, 1 bobble made. In the example, 1 ch. is worked between each bobble. Rep. from * as desired.

Chain lace

This is often used as a foundation for raised and other patterns.
Begin with 29 ch.
1ST ROW: 1 d.c. into 9th ch. from hook, *5 ch., miss 3 ch., 1 d.c. into next ch. Rep. from * to end of ch., 8 ch., turn.
2ND ROW: *1 d.c. into next sp., 5 ch. Rep. from * to end of row, ending with 1 d.c. into last sp., 8 ch., turn. Rep. 2nd row as desired.

Picot lace

Begin with 31 ch.
1ST ROW: 1 d.c. into 3rd ch. from hook (first picot made), 2 ch., 1 d.c. into 8th ch. from picot, *6 ch., 1 d.c. into 3rd ch. from hook (picot made), 2 ch., miss 4 ch., 1 d.c. into next ch. Rep. from * to end of row, 6 ch., turn.
2ND ROW: 1 d.c. into 3rd ch. from hook, 2 ch., 1 d.c. in first sp. to left of picot, *6 ch., 1 d.c. into 3rd ch. from hook, 2 ch., 1 d.c. into next sp. to left of picot. Rep. from * to end of row, 6 ch., turn. Rep. 2nd row as desired.

Double picot lace

Begin with 26 ch.
1ST ROW: 1 d.c. into 3rd ch. from hook (first picot made), 1 ch., 1 d.c. into 7th ch. from picot, *4 ch., 1 d.c. into 3rd ch. from hook, 5 ch., 1 d.c. into 3rd ch. from hook, 1 ch., miss 3 ch. of foundation ch., 1 d.c. into next ch. (1 picot loop made). Rep. picot loops from * as required, 7 ch., turn.
2ND ROW: 1 d.c. into 3rd ch. from hook, 1 ch., 1 d.c. in between picots of first loop, *1 picot loop, 1 d.c. between picots of next loop. Rep. from * working last d.c. into loop after last picot, 6 ch., turn. Rep. 2nd row as desired.

Chevron

Clusters over 1 stitch

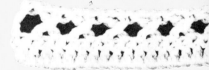

Clusters over 3 stitches

Crossed double trebles

Loop, or poodle, stitch

Chevron   *Illustrated on page 35*
Begin with 42 ch.
1ST ROW: 1 tr. into 3rd ch. from hook, *1 tr. into each of next 5 ch., miss 2 ch., 1 tr. into each of next 5 ch., 3 tr. into next ch. Rep. from *, making only 2 tr. in last ch., 3 ch., turn.
2ND ROW: 1 tr. into base of turning ch. (this increases 1 st.), *5 tr. into each of next 5 tr., miss 2 tr., 5 tr. into each of next 5 tr., 3 tr. into next tr. (centre of 3 tr. group of previous row). Rep. from *, making only 2 tr. in last st. Rep. 2nd row, working in different colours as required.
See p. 31, *Joining colours.*

Clusters   *Illustrated on page 35*
Clusters may be worked into a single stitch, or over several stitches, using trebles, or the longer trebles.

Single stitch cluster
For clarity in the example, 1 ch. has been worked between each cluster. All 3 trs. are worked into same st.
Work 1 tr., leaving last loop on hook (2 loops on hook), work another tr. leaving last loop on hook (3 loops on hook), work another tr. leaving last loop on hook (4 loops on hook), y.o.h. and draw through all loops on hook. 1 cluster made.

Cluster over 3 stitches
Work 1 tr. into each of next 3 trs., leaving the last loop of each on hook, as above, y.o.h. and draw through all loops on hook. 1 cluster made. 3 ch. have been worked between each cluster in the example.

Crossed double trebles   *Illustrated on page 35*
In the example these are worked over a row of treble stitches.
Begin with 6 turning ch., *miss 2 sts., 1 dbl.tr. into next st., 1 ch., inserting hook from behind, work 1 dbl.tr. into the first ch. just missed. 1 crossed treble made. Rep. from * as desired.

Loop, or poodle, stitch *Illustrated on page 35*
This stitch is worked with wrong side facing. When working in rows it is necessary to make 1 row of d.c. between each loop stitch row. If working in circles, the loops may be made continuously.
Begin with a row of d.c. worked over a foundation ch.
*Wrap yarn clockwise once completely round first finger of left hand, keeping finger as close to work as possible, insert hook in next st., then insert it from left to right under the 2 strands of yarn on the finger, draw these through stitch just picked up, y.o.h. and draw through all loops on hook. Remove loop from finger. 1 loop st. made. Rep. from * as desired.

Picot *Illustrated on page 38*
The example begins with 2 rows of tr. sts.
There are various ways of making a picot. The number of chains into which it is made may differ, and sometimes a d.c. is used instead of a s.s. to form the picot.
*3 ch., 1 s.s. (or d.c.) into 3rd ch. from hook, miss 1 st., 1 d.c. into next st. Picot made. Rep. from * as desired.

Shell pattern *Illustrated on page 38*
Begin with 20 ch.
1ST ROW: 2 tr. in 4th ch. from hook, *miss 1 ch., 1 tr. in next ch., miss 1 ch., (3 tr., 2 ch., 3 tr.) in next ch. (shell made). Rep. from * to last 4 ch., miss 1 ch., 1 tr. in next ch., miss 1 ch., 3 tr. in last ch., turn.
2ND ROW: 2 tr. in first st., *1 tr. over tr., (3 tr., 2 ch., 3 tr.) in 2 ch. sp. Rep. from * to last single tr., 1 tr. on tr., 3 tr. in 3rd of 3 turning ch., 3 ch., turn. Rep. 2nd row as desired.

Shell and peak pattern *Illustrated on page 38*
Begin with 24 ch.
1ST ROW: 4 tr. in 4th ch. from hook, *1 ch., miss 3 ch., 5 tr. in next ch., rep. from * to end, 5 ch., turn.
2ND ROW: 1 d.c. in 3rd tr. of 5 tr. group, *2 ch., in next sp. work (1 tr., 1 picot of 3 ch., s.s. into 3rd of 3 ch. from hook, 1 tr.), 2 ch., 1 d.c. in 3rd tr. of 5 tr. group. Rep. from *, 3 ch., turn.
3RD ROW: 5 tr. in first d.c., *1 ch., 5 tr. in next d.c. Rep. from *, 5 ch., turn. Rep. 2nd and 3rd rows as required.

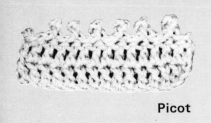

Picot

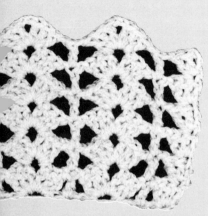

Shell pattern

Shell and peak pattern

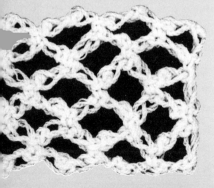

Solomon's knot

Solomon's knot

A very attractive pattern for lacy stoles, scarves, hoods, or sleeves.

1ST ROW: Loop wool over hook, *draw out stitch on hook to form a ½ in. loop, y.o.h. and draw through loop, insert hook into back thread of loop, y.o.h. and draw through first loop, y.o.h. and draw through both loops on hook. 1 Solomon's knot made. Rep. from * as required.

2ND ROW: Miss first 3 Solomon's knots, and work 1 d.c. into centre of next knot, *make 2 knots, miss 1 knot in previous row, 1 d.c. into centre of next knot. Rep. from * to end of row, make 2 knots, turn.

3RD ROW: Work 1 d.c. in knot between d.c.s of previous row, make 2 knots. Rep. to end of row, making last d.c. in last knot, 2 knots, turn.

Rep. 3rd row as required.

Stripes

Worked in contrasting colours, these may be made horizontally or vertically over plain or patterned fabric.

The yarn is always held at the back of the work, the right side facing.

Horizontal stripes

Loop yarn over hook. Holding yarn from ball at the back of work, insert hook from front to back at starting point, y.o.h., and pull through loop on hook. The chain stitches forming the stripes will be worked across the stitches of the fabric, thus: insert hook over next st., y.o.h. and pull through loop on hook. Rep. in straight, or curved, lines as required.

Horizontal picot stripes
These are worked by making 3 ch., 1 s.s. into 3rd ch. from hook between each chain stitch worked across.

Vertical stripes
These are worked similarly to the horizontal, excepting that the stripes are worked parallel to the stitches forming the fabric.

Horizontal stripes

V-pattern

Begin with 25 ch.
1ST ROW: 1 tr. into 3rd ch. from hook, *miss 1 ch., 2 tr. into next ch., rep. from * to end, 3 ch., turn.
2ND ROW: 1 tr. between first 2 tr., *2 tr. between 2 tr. of previous row, rep. from * to end, 3 ch., turn.
Rep. 2nd row as required.

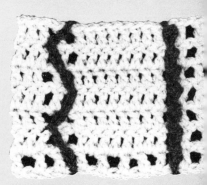

Vertical stripes

Square pattern

Begin with 26 ch.
1ST ROW: 1 tr. into 4th ch. from hook, 1 tr. into each of next 2 ch., *1 ch., miss 1 ch., 1 tr. into each of next 4 ch. Rep. from * to end, 4 ch., turn.
2ND ROW: *1 d.c. into 1 ch. sp. of previous row, 4 ch. Rep. from *, making 1 d.c. into top of turning ch., 3 ch., turn.
3RD ROW: 3 tr. into 1st loop, (1 ch., 4 tr. into next ch. loop) to end of row, 4 ch., turn. Rep. rows 2 and 3 as required.

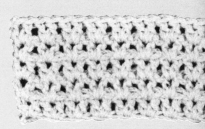

V-pattern

Square pattern

Edgings, borders and insertions

Lacy edgings, borders and insertions can add an extra touch of elegance to so many things. They will enhance all kinds of garments by prettying up neck, sleeves, or hems and can add unique charm to household linen.

With a little practice a beginner will quickly learn this fascinating facet of the craft, and progress to design new ones.

They fall into three main types:

1. Edgings which are worked straight on to material.
2. Edgings and borders which are made separately and sewn, or crocheted, to material.
3. Insertions which are crochet strips to be inset between two pieces of material.

EDGINGS WORKED ON MATERIAL

Before material can be edged it must be prepared by cutting it to correct size. Then draw a thread ¼ in. from the edge, and turn back a narrow hem. The hook will enter the material in the space left by the drawn thread.

To make the foundation row
With right side of material facing, join yarn to one corner, work 3 d.c. into same space, then work d.c. stitches evenly round the sides of the material, making 3 d.c. into each corner. Join with 1 s.s. to first d.c. *Note:* The number of d.c. stitches made must be in multiples which will ensure complete patterns in the rows to follow.

Simple shell and picot edging

To make the picot (pct): 3 ch., 1 s.s. into 3rd ch. from hook.

The edging
**Into 2nd of 3 corner sts. work (3 tr., 1 pct, 3 tr., 1 pct, 3 tr., 1 pct, 3 tr.), miss 2 sts., 1 d.c. in next st., miss 2 sts., *(3 tr., 1 pct, 3 tr.) in next st., miss 2 sts., 1 d.c. in next st., miss 2 sts.* Rep. from * to * to next corner st., then rep. from ** to * all round material. S.s. into 1st tr. of round.
Fasten off yarn.

SOME EDGINGS AND BORDERS
WORKED SEPARATELY

**Plain
picot edging**

1 d.c. in first st., *3 ch., 1 s.s. in 3rd ch. from hook, picot made, miss 1 st., 1 d.c. in next st. Rep. from * to end.

**Bobble-and-peak
edging**

*Y.o.h., insert hook into st., y.o.h. and draw loop up to ½ in. height (or more if desired) 3 or more times into same st., y.o.h. and pull through all loops on hook (1 bobble made), 3 ch., 1 s.s. into 3rd ch. from hook (1 picot made).
Rep. from * as desired.

**Shrimp stitch,
or corded edging**

1ST ROW : Work one row of d.c.
2ND ROW : Work from left to right, instead of right to left; work in d.c., inserting hook under both horizontal threads. The crossed effect obtained forms a beaded type of finish.

**Ribbon
shell edging**

1ST ROW : Work 1 row of d.c., or other stitch, 5 ch., turn.
2ND ROW : *Miss 1 st., 1 dbl.tr. into next st., 1 ch. Rep. from * to end, turn.
3RD ROW : 1 d.c. into first sp., *(1 d.c., 1 tr., 1 d.c.) over first dbl.tr., 1 d.c. in sp.* Rep. from * as desired, ending with 1 d.c. in last sp.

Old English edging

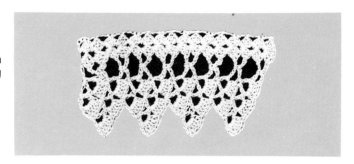

1ST ROW: 14 ch., (3 tr., 1 ch., 3 tr.) in 6th ch. from hook (shell made), 5 ch., miss 4 ch., (1 tr., 3 ch., 1 tr.) in next ch., miss 2 ch., (1 tr., 3 ch., 1 tr.) in last st., 3 ch., turn.

2ND ROW: 4 tr. in next 3 ch. sp., 5 tr. in next 3 ch. sp., 3 ch., 1 d.c. over 5 ch., 3 ch., 1 shell in 1 ch. sp. of previous row, 1 tr. in top of turning ch., 4 ch., turn.

3RD ROW: 1 shell over shell, 5 ch., 1 tr. in first tr. of next 5 tr. group, 3 ch., 1 tr. in same st., (1 tr., 3 ch., 1 tr.) between 2 5-tr. groups, (1 tr., 3 ch., 1 tr.) in top of turning ch., 3 ch., turn.

4TH ROW: 4 tr. in next 3 ch. sp., (5 tr. in next 3 ch. sp.) twice, 3 ch., 1 d.c. over 5 ch., 3 ch., 1 shell over shell, 1 tr. in turning ch., 4 ch., turn.

5TH ROW: 1 shell over shell, 5 ch., 1 tr. in first tr. of next 5 tr. group, 3 ch., 1 tr. in same st., (1 tr., 3 ch., 1 tr.) between first 2 groups of 5 tr., 3 ch., turn.

Rep. rows 2 to 5 as desired.

INSERTION

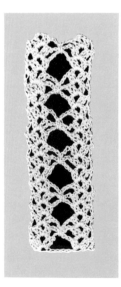

Crochet insertion can be made in any width, using all types of yarn. It may be used horizontally or vertically, to lengthen or widen a garment, or set into material simply as a form of decoration.

Some existing border designs may be adapted as insertions, but the pattern should be symmetrical, and the edges sufficiently even and continuous to allow for perfect joining into the material.

The simple insertion illustrated may be widened by the addition of one or more shells at the beginning and end of the rows, with the appropriate increase in the number of foundation chains.

Instructions for working this simple insertion are given on page 44.

Motif crochet The three motifs pictured here are all made from the same directions. The largest, worked in triple thick wool, measured 10½ in. square; the next, made in thick cotton, measured 5 in. square, and the smallest, in fine cotton, 2½ in. square. (See page 45.)

The sleeveless coat illustrated on page 47 is made up of this motif.

Simple insertion   *Illustrated on page 42*

Begin with 15 ch.

1ST ROW : Into 5th ch. from hook (2 tr., 2 ch., 2 tr.) (shell made), 6 ch., miss 6 ch., 1 shell in next ch., miss 2 ch., 1 tr. in last ch., 3 ch., turn.

2ND ROW : 1 shell over shell in 2 ch., sp., 6 ch., 1 shell over shell in 2 ch., sp., 1 tr. in top of turning ch., 3 ch., turn.

3RD ROW : 1 shell over shell, 3 ch., insert hook under 6th of first row and work 1 d.c. joining 6 ch. of first and second rows to 3rd row, 3 ch., shell over shell, 1 tr. in top of turning ch., 3 ch., turn.

4TH ROW : Shell over shell, 6 ch., shell over shell, 1 tr. in top of turning ch., 3 ch., turn.

Rep. 2nd, 3rd and 4th rows as desired.

For special occasions
An evening bag with a glitter

This attractive evening bag is crocheted in Twilley's Goldfingering. It is easy to make, and instructions are given on page 69.

Motif crochet

Square motifs Motifs, square and round, are among the most popular features in the whole range of modern crochet.

Apart from the elegance they lend to the innumerable articles to which they can be adapted, the reasons for their wide use are no doubt attributable to the fact that the less intricate ones are quick to make and the instructions easy to memorize.

It is surprising how soon a pretty little mat can grow into a cushion cover, or joined with others, could become a priceless tablecloth or bedspread.

Motifs can be made in any type of yarn, in a single colour or in rich blends of shades, according to the artistic inspiration of their creator. For perfect symmetry it is important to use the same thickness of yarn throughout for one article.

The diagram on page 81 will give a good indication of the method of designing a garment made up of motifs. Neck and shoulder shapings are made by working a section of the main motif to the exact size required.

An increase, or reduction, in the size of a garment made up of motifs may often be successfully made by using a larger or smaller hook; working with thicker or thinner yarn; or omitting the last one or two rounds of each motif. Care must be taken that the size of the final garment, worked out according to the exact measurement of each motif, will be correct.

Round motifs

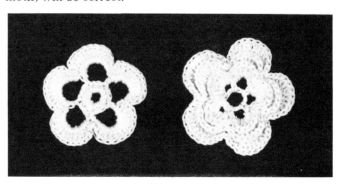

The single or the petalled rose pictured here will add distinction to a dress or suit, belt or Alice band, as well as many household articles.

A single rose, and right, a petalled rose. Instructions for working these charming motifs are given on page 46.

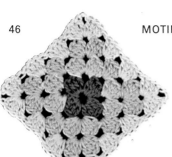

The plain treble-and-chain square, sometimes known as the 'American' or 'Afghan', is a very popular motif. It is used for the bedspread and cushion shown in colour on page 6, for which instructions are given on page 69.

The single rose *Illustrated on page 45*

Begin with 6 ch., join with s.s. into a ring.

1ST ROUND : 15 d.c. into ring, 1 s.s. to first d.c.

2ND ROUND : (7 ch., miss 2 d.c., 1 d.c. into next d.c.) 5 times.

3RD ROUND : Into each 7 ch. loop work (1 d.c., 1 hlf.tr., 10 tr., 1 hlf.tr., 1 d.c.). Fasten off.

The raised petalled rose

Illustrated on page 45

Begin with 8 ch., join with 1 s.s. into a ring.

1ST ROUND : (4 ch., 1 d.c. into ring) 5 times.

2ND ROUND : Into each 4 ch. sp. work (1 d.c., 6 tr., 1 d.c.), 1 s.s. into first d.c.

3RD ROUND : Working from behind 2nd round and between d.c. of first round (6 ch., 1 d.c.) 5 times.

Instructions continued on page 48

When surrounded by chain or picot lace, these rose motifs are very attractive. *Below left*, rose with chain lace, *right*, rose with chain lace and picot edging. Instructions on page 48.

**Top fashion –
the sleeveless coat**

The sleeveless coat is
top fashion, and this one
is made up entirely of
the motif shown on
page 43. Instructions for
making the coat are
given on page 80.

The raised petalled rose *continued*

4TH ROUND: Into each 6 ch. sp. work (1 d.c., 1 hlf.tr., 6 tr., 1 hlf.tr., 1 d.c.). This completes 2 rows of petals.

5TH ROUND: Working from behind 4th round and between d.c. of 3rd round (6 ch., 1 d.c.) 5 times.

6TH ROUND: Into each 6 ch. sp. work (1 d.c., 1 hlf.tr., 7 tr., 1 hlf.tr., 1 d.c.). This completes 3 rows of petals.

Chain lace and picot edging   *Illustrated on page 46*

1ST ROUND: *5 ch., 1 d.c. into centre back of 4th tr. in petal, 5 ch., 1 d.c. into back of last d.c. of same petal. Rep. from * to end of round, joining last 5 ch. with 1 d.c. into back of last d.c. of last petal.

2ND ROUND: S.s. to 3rd ch. of first loop, 1 d.c. in next ch., *6 ch., 1 d.c. in centre of next loop. Rep. from * to end of round. Join with 1 s.s. to first d.c.

3RD ROUND: Rep. 2nd round, making 7 ch. loops.

FURTHER ROUNDS: Rep. 2nd round, increasing each loop by 1 ch. as necessary.

LAST ROUND(S): A neat finish is made by working 7 d.c. (or more according to size of last round of loops) into every ch. loop.

PICOT ROUND: A 3 ch. picot made into alternate d.c.s of previous round gives an attractive edging.

JOINING MOTIFS

Joining square motifs   A neat oversewn, or flat seam, made on the wrong side, makes a satisfactory join. A double-crocheted seam, worked on either the right or the wrong side, is often used. Seams are fully described and illustrated on pages 91 and 92.

When a number of multi-coloured squares are to be joined, an attractive effect is obtained by working the outer edges of each motif in the same colour, and then making the double-crochet joins in one of the contrasting colours.

Joining round motifs   Make one motif, then on the last round of a second motif join it to the first one with a slip stitch at various points. They can also be sewn together.

Another way is to join by making 'filling' motifs. See the 'Duchesse' set on page 72.

Using ring motifs These are worked on ordinary curtain rings. Instructions for covering and joining rings are given on page 21. Here are instructions for making a gay set of accessories using ring motifs.

Belt *Materials:* 1 spool each of Twilley Goldfingering in main and contrast colour
61 1 in. diameter plastic curtain rings
No. 12 (2·50 mm) crochet hook
Size: to fit 25 in. waist. If a larger, or smaller, size is required, add, or deduct, the necessary rings.

Method: Cover 40 rings in main shade and 21 in contrast. Join main colour rings together in 2 lines of 20. Join contrast rings together in 1 line. Sew contrast line in centre of main lines, fitting contrast rings alternately. Using 4 strands of contrast, make 2 crochet chains join to each end of belt.

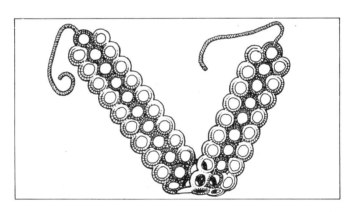

Matching neckband *Materials:* 2 balls Twilley Goldfingering
15 1 in. diameter curtain rings
No. 12 (2·50 mm) crochet hook
When covered, arrange rings as in the illustration.

BAND
Begin with 6 ch.
1ST ROW: 1 d.c. into 2nd ch. from hook, 1 d.c. into each ch., 1 ch., turn.
2ND ROW: 1 d.c. into each d.c. to end, 1 ch., turn.
Rep. 2nd row for 11 in., or length required. Fasten off. Join with Velcro, or press fastener.

Hairpin crochet

Hairpin crochet is made, as its name suggests, on a U-shaped instrument. At one time it was quite usual for a woman to extract a hairpin from her coiffure and proceed to make strips of this special kind of crochet, or 'gimp', as it is called. On completion, the hairpin would revert to its original function, and she would crochet together the results of her handiwork.

The modern hairpin is functionally designed in various widths, from the smallest, $\frac{1}{2}$ in. wide, to cope with the finest cottons, to the largest, 3 in. wide, for other types of yarns.

The general working principle is the same throughout. Variations in pattern are obtained by the different ways of forming the central 'spine' of each length of gimp, and in the many ways of joining the strips together. This central spine is worked with a crochet hook.

The illustration shows, left to right, a simple gimp with a thread through the loops on one side; the first variation: 1 ch., 1 tr. centre; the second variation: open centre; and the third variation: a ribbon bar centre. Instructions for working these are given on page 52.

General hints

When making the strips, the loops should rest easily, but not too tightly, on the prongs of the hairpin. If the hairpin is held with the opening at the top, it will be easier to move the hook as the hairpin is turned.

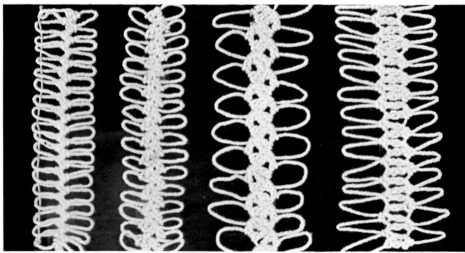

Fringed strip

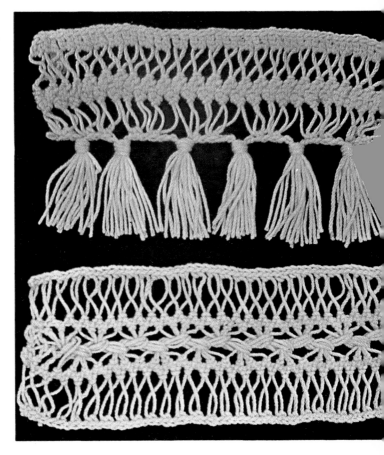

3-loop woven join

Instructions for joining the strips are on page 53

Before a long strip of loops is removed from the hairpin, run a piece of contrasting yarn through the loops on one side and tie the ends loosely. This will ensure that these loops will not twist together while the other side is being joined up.

Almost anything, the finest gossamer-like stoles, trimmings, household articles, and garments of all kinds, can be made quickly in this attractive manner.

The following instructions giving the basic techniques and variations will lead the crocheter to more ambitious ventures, either by the use of more advanced published directions, or by working out individual designs.

WORKING METHOD

A simple gimp The following instructions for a simple gimp will give excellent practice in the basic technique.

Working method   Hold the crochet hook in right hand. Make a loop at the end of yarn and slip this on to the hook.

Hold the hairpin in the left hand between thumb and first finger, with the open end at the top, and the squared base in the hand, and proceed as follows.

1. With the loop on the hook, wind yarn round right prong of hairpin.
2. Yarn over hook and draw through loop on hook, keeping the loop at centre of hairpin (44).
3. Raise hook to a vertical position and turn hairpin to the left (45).
4. Yarn over hook and draw through loop on hook (46).
5. Insert hook into loop on left prong, yarn over hook (47), and draw loop through (2 loops on hook), yarn over hook and draw through the 2 loops on hook (1 d.c. made).

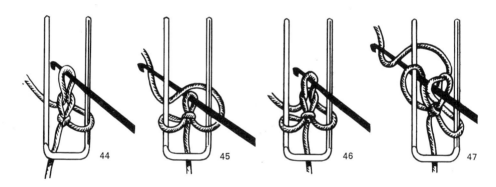

Repeat stages 3 to 5 until hairpin is filled with loops. Remove all loops, and then replace the last 3 or 4 loops on to the correct prongs and continue working as required.

Centre of gimp:
variations
Illustrated on page 50

1 ch., 1 tr. centre
Instead of making the d.c., work 1 ch., 1 tr. into front of loop.

Open centre
Instead of the d.c., work 1 ch., then (1 tr., 2 ch., 1 tr.) into front of loop.

Ribbon bars
Make 4 ch. between every d.c. into loop. If preferred 1 slip stitch may be substituted for d.c.

Finishing off the strips There are many ways of doing this. The following suggestion is given as a guide. Instructions are for a single strip finished with a tasselled fringe along one edge.

Make a length of gimp with any chosen centre.

For the heading Along one side of gimp work 2 tr. into every loop, giving each loop one twist, all in the same direction.

For the lower edge *1 d.c. into 2 loops taken together, 1 ch., 1 d.c. into next 2 loops together, 5 ch. Rep. from * to end of loops.

To attach the fringe Take the required number of strands of yarn, fold in half, and insert hook through 5 ch. sp., draw through the opening the central loop of strands, then draw the fringe ends through this loop. Pull up the tassel tightly. Continue as required.

Joining the strips The strips may be joined in one colour, or in one or more contrasting shades.

A simple method Join yarn to first loop. Giving every loop one twist (all in the same direction), insert hook into first loop of first strip on the left, 1 ch., then insert hook into first loop of strip on the right, taking 1 loop in this way from left to right to end of strips. Fasten off securely.

Weaving edges together Without using any yarn, insert hook in 1 or more loops on the left, and draw through the same number of loops on the right, then on the left, and so on to the end of the loops. Fasten off securely.

When all the strips are joined together, the outer edges may be finished off in many ways.

A simple finish *Give each loop one twist (always twist loops in the same direction), insert hook into loop and work 1 d.c. Rep. from * to end of loops.

If a more open edge is preferred, 1 ch. may be added between each d.c.

Picots and other decorative edgings may be worked into the loops as desired.

Tunisian crochet

Tunisian crochet, sometimes known as Tricot or Afghan crochet, is quick and easy to do, and its products are very firm, practical and attractive.

Bath mats, blankets and cot covers are among the many useful things which can be made in Tunisian crochet, by using single width or strips sewn or crocheted together, in plain or blended colours.

The special hook For this effective crochet, a long hook is used, of uniform thickness from the hooked end along the shank to the knobbed end. A Tunisian hook is shown on page 11. The hook should be slightly longer than the width of the work, to allow for comfortable working.

Working hints Every row is crocheted from right to left, retaining all the stitches on the hook, and without turning the work, they are then gradually taken off from left to right.

Instruction leaflets usually refer to the taking-up and taking-off rows as one complete row, as in the following directions. Sometimes, however, this row is divided into 1st and 2nd rows.

As in ordinary crochet, special attention must be paid to *working into all end stitches,* and the counting habit should be cultivated.

The following patterns are exercises in the basic techniques of Tunisian crochet. After a little practice, other variations will quickly spring to mind.

Plaited Tunisian crochet. Working instructions are given on page 56.

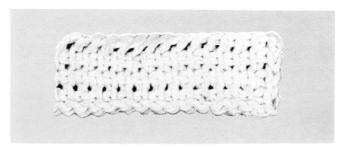

Plain Tunisian Begin with the required length of chain.

1ST ROW: Insert hook in 2nd ch. from hook, y.o.h., and draw yarn through, keeping loop on hook. *Insert hook into next ch., y.o.h. and draw through, keeping this loop also on hook. Rep. from * to end of ch.

To take loops off: Y.o.h., and draw through first loop on hook, **y.o.h., and draw through 2 loops on hook. Rep. from ** to last loop on hook.

2ND ROW: The loop on hook forms the first stitch of the new row. Insert hook from right to left through 2nd upright st. in previous row, y.o.h. and draw yarn through, keeping loop on hook, *insert hook from right to left through next upright stitch, y.o.h. and draw yarn through, keeping this loop on hook. Rep. from * to end of row.

To take loops off: Y.o.h. and draw through first loop, **y.o.h. and draw through 2 loops on hook. Rep. from ** to end. Rep. 2nd row as required.

LAST ROW: 1 s.s. into each upright stitch of last row worked.

Open Tunisian Begin with a length of chain.

1ST ROW: Miss first ch., insert hook in next ch., y.o.h. and draw through. Keep this loop on hook. *Insert hook into next ch., y.o.h. and draw through, keeping this loop on hook. Rep. from * to end of row. Y.o.h., draw through first

continued overleaf

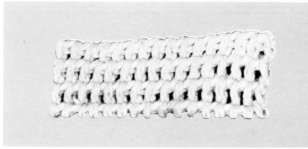

Open Tunisian

Open Tunisian   loop on hook, **y.o.h. and draw through 2 loops on hook. Rep. from ** to end.

There is now a row of small horizontal stitches at the back along top of row. These are the stitches to be worked into.

2ND ROW : Insert hook into horizontal stitch at back of 2nd upright stitch in previous row, y.o.h. and draw through, *insert hook into horizontal stitch at back of next upright st., y.o.h. and pull through. Rep. from * to end. Y.o.h. and draw through first loop on hook, **y.o.h. and draw through 2 loops on hook. Rep. from ** to end. Rep. 2nd row as required.

LAST ROW : As for plain Tunisian.

Plaited Tunisian   Begin with a length of chain.
Illustrated on page 54   1ST ROW : Work as for first row of plain Tunisian.

2ND ROW : Insert hook from right to left through 3rd upright stitch, y.o.h. and draw through, insert hook through 2nd upright stitch (just missed), y.o.h. and draw through, *miss 1 upright stitch, insert hook in next upright stitch, y.o.h. and draw through, insert hook through the stitch missed, y.o.h. and draw through. Rep. from * until 1 upright stitch remains, insert hook through this stitch, y.o.h. and draw through; y.o.h. and draw through first loop on hook, **y.o.h. and draw through 2 loops on hook. Rep. from * to end. Rep. 2nd row as required.

LAST ROW : As for plain Tunisian.

SHAPING TUNISIAN CROCHET

To decrease   Insert hook from right to left through 2 upright stitches, y.o.h. and pull through both loops together.

To increase   At the beginning of a row, insert hook from right to left through first upright stitch, y.o.h. and draw through, then continue along row as for plain Tunisian to last upright stitch. Insert hook into stitch between last 2 upright stitches, y.o.h. and pull through, insert hook into last upright stitch, y.o.h. and draw through.

Filet crochet

Filet, the French word for net, is an apt name for this most useful, yet very simple, block-and-space type of crochet. Its popularity, which has persisted from early times to the present day, may well be attributed to the fact that it can easily be worked from a simple chart with very few words of instruction.

In the past, this type of crochet was used mainly for the adornment of household linen; it also featured in ecclesiastical lace; but today it is widely used for many things, in any yarn, and in any hook size.

An experienced crocheter will have no difficulty in working out a chart for a favourite design – a flower, initials, names or even dates – for a really personal memento.

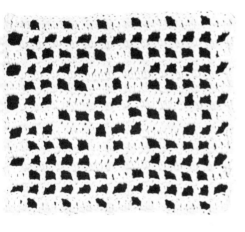

The illustration shows a simple geometrical design worked from the accompanying chart. Each black square on the chart represents one block of trebles; each white square represents a space. When working a single block, 4 treble stitches are made; for 2 adjoining blocks, 7 trebles; for 3, 10 trebles, and so on.

The first two rows of this filet square are given in the conventional manner. By comparison, the time-saving chart technique will be seen to have many advantages.

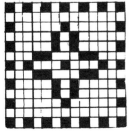

The first two rows
Begin with 42 ch.
1ST ROW : 1 tr. in 4th ch. from hook, 1 tr. in each of next 2 ch., *2 ch., miss 2 ch., 1 tr. in each of next 4 ch. Rep. from * to last ch., 6 ch., turn.
2ND ROW : 1 tr. over last tr. of first block, *2 ch., miss 2 sts., 1 tr. over 1st tr. of next block, 2 ch., miss 2 sts., 1 tr. over last tr. of same block. Rep. from * to end of row, 3 ch., turn.

58

Beads and other trimmings

Beaded crochet

Beads are sometimes used to enhance crochet work, and it is much easier to attach them as the stitches are formed.

Thread the required number of beads on to the yarn before each ball is begun, and bring a bead up between the stitches as the pattern instructs.

Tassels Wind the yarn round a piece of cardboard slightly deeper than the finished length of tassel. Thread a length of yarn through the top and draw loops closely together, tie tightly and leave the loose ends for attaching later. Cut loops at the other end, and wind another length of yarn just below the tied end to shape the tassel. Trim ends evenly.

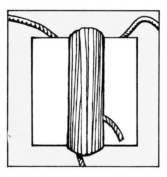

Fringes For a simple fringe, cut the yarn into equal lengths. Taking up the required number of threads, place hook from back to front on the edge of work, fold threads in half and place fold over hook. Pull hook back through stitch and fold ends of fringe over hook, drawing them through loop on hook. (A rug hook makes the action easier.) Knot neatly. Repeat at regular intervals.

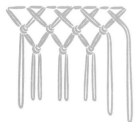

A more elaborate fringe may be made by threading the number of lengths required as shown in the diagram, and knotting as illustrated.

Twisted cord Use several lengths of yarn approximately three times as long as the required finished size, and knot a loop at each end. If a friend is not available to hold one end, it can be slipped over a hook or a door handle.

Place a pencil, or similar object, inside the loop at the hand-holding end, and stand away from the attached end, so that the threads are taut.

Twist the pencil round and round until the cord tightens. Place both ends together and allow the cord to twist round itself evenly. Tie or knot each end.

Pom-pons

Cut two 2 in. (or larger) circles of card and make a ½ in. hole in centre of each piece and a slit from centre to edge of cards (A).

Using a wool needle with two or three long strands of yarn, thread yarn over card circles until the hole is filled (B).

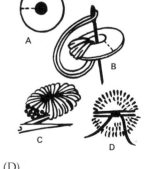

With a sharp pair of scissors, and working between the cards, cut round outer edge of circles (C).

Tie another length of yarn round the centre with a secure knot, leaving the ends for tying later to twisted cord or other work (D).

Pull out the cards carefully, as they can be used repeatedly. Trim pom-pon to a good shape.

Patterns and pattern reading

Choosing a pattern Crocheters can choose from a wide variety of patterns, but a word of caution is necessary for beginners, who would be wise to start with something simple in an easy stitch which can be quickly completed.

Pattern reading Patterns available today cover everything that can be made in crochet, yet the joys of making these beautiful things elude many people who find it difficult to read patterns.

All good patterns clearly define any particular pattern or stitch, and always list the abbreviations used. Some also picture the stitch in actual size, and this is a helpful guide.

Before starting a piece of crochet, the abbreviations should be carefully studied, and the general directions thoroughly understood.

The usual abbreviations The following are the more usual abbreviations:

ch.	chain	y.o.h.	yarn over hook
d.c.	double crochet	sp(s)	space(s)
tr.	treble	blk	block
hlf.tr.	half treble	cl.	cluster
dbl.tr.	double treble	lp(s)	loop(s)
trip.tr.	triple treble	pct(s)	picot(s)
quad.tr.	quadruple treble	rep.	repeat
quin.tr.	quintuple treble	in.	inch(es)
s.s. *or*	slip stitch, *or*	st.(s)	stitch(es)
s.c.	single crochet		

The following symbols are also used:

* asterisk: repeat instructions after the * as many times as stated
( ) parenthesis: repeat instructions within the brackets the number of times stated.

Measurements Many garment patterns give instructions for making several sizes. Before beginning the work, go through the pattern and clearly underline the instructions for the size to be made. This will help to avoid mistakes.

Directions for the smallest size are usually given first, followed by the others in brackets.

Adjusting pattern directions

If it is necessary to lengthen or shorten the article being made, the alterations should be noted on the pattern before work begins. Yarn requirements can also be adjusted at this stage.

Adjustments to body measurements should be made before reaching the shaping for the armhole and the hips.

In some fashion-wear the skirts are worked from the waist downwards. This helps to cope with garments for growing children, as well as the ever-changing hemline, for a skirt worked in this way makes the addition or subtraction of several rows a simple operation.

Reversible patterns

Some patterns in crochet are reversible, while others, such as clusters and loop stitch, have a definite one-sided appearance.

In circular work, one-sided patterns are continuous. When working in rows, it is necessary either to work the particular one-sided row when the correct side faces the worker, or to break off the yarn at the end of the row, and re-join it at the other end, in readiness for the next row.

Loop stitch
right side

Loop stitch
wrong side

Instructions for working loop stitch are given on page 37.

Things to make

By now you should be able to work confidently all the basic crochet stitches, so here is a selection of things to make for yourself or the family. Read all the instructions through carefully before you begin, and make sure you understand all the abbreviations. Buy the yarn recommended, in the quantity given, and be sure to work the tension check – it is most important. If there are less stitches to one inch than the pattern requires, use a finer hook; if there are more, change to a larger hook.

A charming dress in several sizes

A suit in a simple stitch

Instructions for working these garments are given overleaf

A charming dress in several sizes *Illustrated on page 62*

Materials:
Motoravia Double Knitting or
Lorette Double Crepe or
Super Bri-Nylon Double Knitting
5   5   7   13   15   17 balls
One 4 in. zip for sizes 22, 24, 26 in.
One 5 in. zip for sizes 32, 34, 36 in.
1 crochet hook No. 7 (4·50 mm)
1 crochet hook No. 6 (5·00 mm)

Measurements:
Chest or Bust:
22; 24; 26; 32; 34; 36 in.
Length from top of shoulder:
15 (17; 20; 30; 32; 34) or as required

Tension:
4 d.c. to one inch using No. 7 hook (*measured over pressed fabric*).
Check tension. If there are less d.c. to one inch than the number stated, change to a finer hook. If more, change to a larger hook.

Abbreviations:

alt.	alternate	inc.	increase(ing)
beg.	beginning	in.	inch(es)
comm.	commencement	rem.	remain(ing)
cont.	continue(uity)	rep.	repeat
ch.	chain	sl.	slip
dec.	decreasing	st(s).	stitch(es)
d.c.	double crochet	tog.	together
foll(s).	follow(s)(ing)	tr.	treble

L.T.   long treble – wool twice over hook, insert hook into stitch, wool over hook, draw through one loop (wool over hook, draw through 2 loops) 3 times.

Follow first set of figures for 22 in. chest; follow first set of figures in brackets for 24 in. chest; follow second set of figures in brackets for 26 in. chest; follow third set of figures in brackets for 32 in. bust; follow fourth set of figures in brackets for 34 in. bust; and follow fifth set of figures in brackets for 36 in. bust. When only one set of figures given, this applies to all sizes.

YOKE (*The dress is worked from neck to hem*)
Using No. 7 hook, make 49 (53; 57; 69; 73; 77) ch.
1st row: 1 d.c. in 2nd ch. from hook, 1 d.c. in each rem. ch. 48 (52; 56; 68; 72; 76) d.c.

2nd row: 1 d.c. in each of first 2 (4; 7; 6; 1; 2) d.c., * 2 d.c. in next d.c., 1 d.c. in each of next 2 (2; 2; 3; 4; 4) d.c., rep. from * to last 4 (6; 7; 6; 1; 4) d.c., 2 d.c. in next d.c., 1 d.c. in each rem. d.c. 63 (67; 71; 83; 87; 91) d.c.
3rd and every alt. row: 1 d.c. in each d.c. to end.
4th row: 1 d.c. in each of first 3 (6; 7; 5; 9; 4) d.c., * 2 d.c. in next d.c., 1 d.c. in each of next 3 (3; 3; 4; 4; 5) d.c., rep. from * to last 4 (5; 8; 8; 8; 3) d.c., 2 d.c. in next d.c., 1 d.c. in each rem. d.c. 78 (82; 86; 98; 102; 106) d.c.
6th row: 1 d.c. in each of first 4 (5; 1; 6; 1; 3) d.c., * 2 d.c. in next d.c., 1 d.c. in each of next 4 (4; 5; 5; 6; 6) d.c., rep. from * to last 4 (7; 1; 8; 3; 5) d.c., 2 d.c. in next d.c., 1 d.c. in each rem. d.c. 93 (97; 101; 113; 117; 121) d.c.
8th row: 1 d.c. in each of first 4 (6; 1; 1; 3; 5) d.c., * 2 d.c. in next d.c., 1 d.c. in each of next 5 (5; 6; 7; 7; 7) d.c., rep. from * to last 5 (7; 2; 1; 2; 4) d.c., 2 d.c. in next d.c., 1 d.c. in each rem. d.c. 108 (112; 116; 128; 132; 136) d.c.
10th row: 1 d.c. in each of first 2 (4; 6; 5; 7; 9) d.c., * 2 d.c. in next d.c., 1 d.c. in each of next 7 (7; 7; 8; 8; 8) d.c., rep. from * to last 2 (4; 6; 8; 10) d.c., 2 d.c. in next d.c., 1 d.c. in each rem. d.c. 122 (126; 130; 142; 146; 150) d.c.
Work 2 (2; 3; 4; 4; 4) rows without shaping.
Using a damp cloth and warm iron, press the yoke carefully into a circular shape.

SKIRT
Using the No. 6 hook:
1st row: 3 ch. (to count as 1st tr.) * (1 tr., 1 ch., 1 tr.) in 2nd d.c., miss 1 d.c., 1 tr. in next d.c., miss 1 d.c., rep. from * 4 (4; 4; 5; 5; 6) times, make 13 (13; 13; 16; 19; 19) (very loosely) ch., miss next 23 d.c., [1 tr. in next d.c., (1 tr., 1 ch., 1 tr.) in next d.c., miss next d.c.] 9 (10; 11; 12; 13; 12) times, 13 (13; 13; 16; 19; 19) (very loosely) ch., miss next 23 d.c., [1 tr. in next d.c., miss next d.c., (1 tr., 1 ch., 1 tr.) in next d.c., miss next d.c.] 5 (5; 5; 6; 6; 7) times, miss next d.c., 1 tr. on end d.c., 3 ch., turn. 19 (20; 21; 24; 25; 26) blocks of (1 tr., 1 ch., 1 tr.).
2nd row: (2 L.T., 1 ch., 2 L.T.) in first (1 tr., 1 ch., 1 tr.) sp. (1 bell made), * 1 bell in next (1 tr., 1 ch., 1 tr.) sp., rep. from * 3 (3; 3; 4; 4; 5) times, work 1 tr. in each ch. of preceding row, 1 bell in each (1 tr., 1 ch., 1 tr.) sp. to second set of ch., work 1 tr. in each of these ch., 1 bell in next 5 (5; 5; 6; 6; 7) (1 tr., 1 ch., 1 tr.) sp., 1 tr. in end tr., 3 ch., turn.

continued on page 77

A suit in a simple stitch *Illustrated on page 63*

Measurements:
JACKET: 34 (36) [38] in. bust
Length from shoulder: 21 (21) [21] in.
Length of undersleeve seam: 16 (16) [16] in.
SKIRT: 36 (38) [40] in. hip
24 (26) [28] in. waist
Length: 21 (21) [21] in., or as required.

Tension: 9 sts. to 2 in. (No. 8 (4·00 mm) crochet hook.)

Abbreviations:

ch.	chain	d.c.	double crochet
sts.	stitches	sl.	slip
tr.	treble	in.	inches

Materials

JACKET	34	36	38 in. bust
Lister Bel Air Double			
Crochet Yarn	23	24	25 balls
Lister Lavenda			
Double Crepe	21	22	23 ozs
Lister Bri-Nylon			
Double Knitting	23	24	25 balls
SKIRT	36	38	40 in. hip
Lister Bel Air Double			
Crochet Yarn	14	15	16 balls
Lister Lavenda			
Double Crepe	13	14	15 ozs
Lister Bri-Nylon			
Double Knitting	14	15	16 balls

Crochet hooks Nos. 8 (4·00 mm), and
9 (3·50 mm)
11 buttons; ¾ (1) [1] yd (68·6 (91·4) [91·4] cms)
elastic for waist.

JACKET
For 36 in. bust follow figures in parenthesis ( ).
For 38 in. bust follow figures in brackets [ ].

Back
Using No. 8 crochet hook, ch. 84 (88) [92].
1st row: 1 tr. into 2nd ch. from hook, * 1 d.c.
into next ch., 1 tr. into next ch., rep. from * to
end, 1 ch., turn.
2nd row: * 1 tr. into 1 d.c. of previous row,
1 d.c. into tr. of previous row, rep. from * to
end, ending 1 tr. into turning ch., 1 ch., turn.
Repeat 2nd row until work measures 13 (13)
[13] in. from commencement.

Shape armholes Right side facing:
1st row: Sl.st. across first 6 (8) [10] sts., pattern
to last 6 (8) [10] sts., 1 ch., turn.

2nd row: Work in pattern.
3rd row: Sl.st. across 2 sts., pattern to last 2 sts.,
1 ch., turn.
4th row: Work in pattern.
Rep. last 2 rows once more. Continue straight
until work measures 21 (21) [21] in.

Shape shoulders Right side facing:
1st row: Sl.st. across first 6 sts., pattern to last
6 sts., turn.
Rep. last row twice more. Fasten off.

Left Front
Using No. 8 crochet hook, ch. 42 (46) [50].
Work in pattern as Back until work measures
13 (13) [13] in. from commencement.

Shape armhole Right side facing:
1st row: Sl.st. across first 6 (8) [10] sts., pattern
to end, 1 ch., turn.
2nd row: Work in pattern.
3rd row: Sl.st. across first 2 sts., pattern to end,
1 ch., turn.
4th row: Work in pattern.
Rep. last 2 rows once more. Continue straight
until work measures 19½ (19½) [19½] in. from
commencement.

Shape neck Wrong side facing:
Next row: Sl.st. across first 7 (9) [11] sts.,
pattern to end.
Next row: Pattern to last st., turn.
Next row: Sl.st. across 1 st., pattern to end,
1 ch., turn. Continue thus decreasing 1 st. at
neck edge on every row until 18 sts. remain.
Continue on these sts. until work measures
21 (21) [21] in. from commencement.

Shape shoulder
Commencing at armhole edge, sl.st. across 6
sts. at beginning of next and following 2 rows.
Fasten off.

Right Front
Work as Left Front, reversing all shapings.

Sleeves
Using No. 8 crochet hook, ch. 38 (42) [46] and
work in pattern as Back for 4 (4) [4] rows.
Now increase 1 st. at each end of next and
following 4th row until there are 60 (64) [68] sts.
Continue on these sts. until work measures 16
(16) [16] in. *continued on page 68*

This lacy summer jumper is easy to crochet

Materials:

For bust sizes:	34	36	38	40 in.
Motoravia Double Knitting	11	12	13	14 balls
Bri-nylon Double Knitting	11	12	13	14 balls
Leemont Double Crepe	10	11	12	13 ozs

Crochet hooks Nos. 8 (4·00 mm),
7 (4·50 mm) and
9 (3·00 mm)

Measurements:

For bust sizes:	34	36	38	40 in.
Length from top of shoulder	19½	20	20½	21 in.

Tension:
3 patterns to 4 in. using No. 7 hook. (1 patt. consists of one 5 tr. blk. and one single tr.)

Abbreviations:

blk.	block	rep.	repeat
ch.	chain	st(s).	stitches
d.c.	double crochet	sp.	space
in.	inches	tr.	treble
sl.st.	slip stitch	patt.	pattern

Follow first set of figures for 34 in. size; follow first set of figures in brackets for 36 in. size; follow second set of figures in brackets for 38 in. size; follow third set of figures in brackets for 40 in. size. When only one set of figures is given, this applies to all sizes.

FRONT

Using No. 8 hook make 73 (79; 85; 91) ch.
1st row: 5 tr. into 4th ch. from hook (one 5 tr. blk. made), miss 2 ch., 1 tr. in next ch., * miss 2 ch., one 5 tr. blk. in next ch., miss 2 ch., 1 tr. in next ch., rep. from * to last 3 ch., miss 2 ch., 1 tr. in end ch., 3 ch. turn (to count as first tr. on next row). 12 (13; 14; 15) 5 tr. blks.
2nd row: Miss first tr., 1 d.c., 2 ch., 1 d.c. into centre tr. of first 5 tr. blk. (one 2 ch. sp. made), * 1 ch., 1 d.c. on top of next single tr. of previous row, 1 ch., one 2 ch. sp. in centre of next 5 tr. blk., rep. from * to end, working 1 ch., 1 d.c. on end ch. of previous row, 3 ch., turn, which counts as first tr. on next row.
3rd row: Miss first tr., 5 tr. blk. in centre of first 2 ch. sp., * 1 tr. on single d.c. of previous row, 5 tr. blk. in centre of next 2 ch. sp., rep. from * to end, working 1 ch., 1 tr. on end d.c. of previous row, 3 ch., turn, which counts as first d.c. of next row.
The 2nd and 3rd rows form the patt. throughout.
Cont. in patt. until work measures 3 in. from comm.
Using No. 7 hook, proceed in patt. until work measures 13 in. (or desired length to underarm) ending after a 3rd patt. row, no ch. to turn after last row.

Shape armholes
Sl.st. over first 6 trs., 1 ch., one 2 ch. sp. in centre of next 5 tr. blk., patt. to last 5 tr. blk. and single tr., 3 ch., turn. 10 (11; 12; 13) 5 tr. blks.
Cont. without further shaping until work measures 18½ (19; 19½; 20) in. from comm. ending after a 3rd patt. row.

continued on page 86

New sleeves for old

These crochet sleeves will liven up an old dress, or add a formal touch to a sleeveless top.

Materials:
For bust measurements: 33 (35) [37] in.
Bel Air Starspun   4   5   5 balls
    (for sleeves only)

Crochet hooks Nos. 12 (2·50 mm),
                    10 (3·00 mm),
                    9 (3·50 mm),
                    8 (4·00 mm),
                    7 (4·50 mm) and
                    6 (5·00 mm)

Measurements:
Length of undersleeve seam: 17 in. for all sizes.

Abbreviations:

sts. stitches	ch. chain
in. inches	tr. treble
d.c. double crochet	

For 35 in. bust size follow figures in ( ).
For 37 in. bust size follow figures in [ ].

With No. 12 crochet hook work 63 (71) [71] ch.
1st row: 1 d.c. into 7th ch. from hook, * 5 ch., miss 3 ch., 1 d.c. into next ch., repeat from * to end, 3 ch., turn.
2nd row: 3 tr. into first d.c., * 1 d.c. into next loop, 5 ch., 1 d.c. into next loop, 3 tr. into next d.c., repeat from * ending 1 d.c. into turning ch. loop, 7 ch., turn.
3rd row: 1 d.c. into centre tr. of 3 tr. group, * 5 ch., 1 d.c. into next loop, 5 ch., 1 d.c. into centre tr. of next 3 tr. group, repeat from * to end, 7 ch., turn.
4th row: 1 d.c. into first loop, * 3 tr. into next d.c., 1 d.c. into next loop, 5 ch., 1 d.c. into next loop, repeat from * to end, 7 ch., turn.
5th row: 1 d.c. into first loop, * 5 ch., 1 d.c. into centre tr. of next 3 tr. group, 5 ch., 1 d.c. into next loop, repeat from * to end, 3 ch., turn.

The last 4 rows from 2nd–5th inclusive form the pattern. Continue in pattern until work measures 3 (3) [3] in. from commencement, then **change to No. 10 hook** and continue until work measures 6 (6) [6] in. from commencement. **Change to No. 9 hook** and continue until work measures 9 (9) [9] in. from commencement, then **change to No. 8 hook** and continue until work

measures 13 (13) [13] in. from commencement. **Change to No. 7 hook** and continue until work measures 16 (16) [16] in. from commencement.

For 33 in. bust size change to No. 6 hook and work a further 2½ in. in pattern. Fasten off.

(For 35 in. bust size continue on No. 7 hook for a further 2¾ in. pattern and fasten off.)

[For 37 in. bust size change to No. 6 hook and work 3 in. in pattern and fasten off.]

For sleeve seam, join on yarn to 1st ch. of basic ch. at beginning. Hold the two sides close together and using No. 12 hook work 2 ch., then 1 d.c. into other end of basic ch. 2 ch., 1 d.c. into first side edge ¼ in. up from lower edge. * 2 ch., 1 d.c. into other side ¼ in. above previous d.c., 2 ch., 1 d.c. into first side ¼ in. above previous d.c., continue joining in this way until 2½ (2¾) [3] in. from top of Sleeve, now continue joining for a further 1 in. but working only 1 ch. between the d.c. Fasten off leaving last 1½ (1¾) [2] in. open.

See page 94 for general washing instructions. Do not use an enzyme washing powder which removes stains. Dry away from direct heat, and if pressing is desired use a cool iron over a dry cloth. Press lightly.

A tablecloth to treasure *Illustrated on frontispiece*

Materials:
20 ozs 23 25-grm. balls Twilley's Lyscordet
Stratnoid crochet hook No. 12 (2·50 mm).

Measurements: The finished cloth is 48 in.
square.

Tension: 1 motif measures 4 in.
Check the tension by working 2 motifs or
working the first 3 (4) rounds. If the tension is
tight, use a size larger hook, if loose use a finer
hook.

Abbreviations: see page 60.

1st MOTIF
Commence with 5 ch., s.s. into 1st ch. to form a
ring.
1st round: 3 ch., 15 tr. into ring, s.s. into 3rd of
3 ch.
2nd round: 6 ch. (1 dbl.tr., 2 ch.) into each tr.,
s.s. into 4th of 6 ch.
3rd round: 3 d.c., into 2 ch. sp., s.s. into 1st d.c.
4th round: 3 ch., leaving last lp. of each dbl.tr.
on hook, make 1 dbl.tr. into each of next 3 d.c.,
yarn over hook and draw through all lps. on
hook, 5 ch., * leaving last lp. of each dbl.tr. on
hook, make 1 dbl.tr. into same place as last
dbl.tr., and into each of next 3 d.c., yarn over
hook and draw through all lps. on hook (a 4 tr.
cluster formed), 5 ch., rep. from * ending with
s.s. into 3rd of 3 ch. Fasten off (16 clusters).

2nd MOTIF
Work as for 1st motif until 4th round is
reached.
4th round: Work beginning and rep. of 4th
round as 1st motif once, * 4 tr. cluster over
same d.c. as last dbl.tr., and over next 3 d.c.,
2 ch., 1 d.c. into 3rd of appropriate 5 ch. lp. on
1st motif, 2 ch., rep. from * once more, complete
as for 1st motif.
Continue joining motifs as before and make a
square of 12 motifs by 12.

FILLING
Same as for 1st motif until 1st round is completed.
2nd round: 1 d.c. into 1st tr., * 3 ch., 1 d.c.
into 3rd ch. of appropriate 5 ch. lp. on a motif,
3 ch., miss 1 tr., 1 d.c. into next tr. on filling;
rep. from * omitting last d.c. of last rep.; s.s.
into 1st d.c. Fasten off.

EDGING
With right side facing, attach yarn to first
5 ch.lp. after a motif join, 3 d.c. into same lp.,
3 ch.s.s. into 1st ch. (a picot formed), 3 d.c. into
same lp., *** into next lp., work 3 d.c., 3 ch.,
s.s. into 1st ch., 3 d.c. rep. from * into each
5 ch.lp., until next motif join is reached, 3 d.c.
into each of next 2 lps., rep. from ** ending
with s.s. into 1st d.c. Fasten off.

Suit *continued from page 65*

Shape sleevehead
1st row: Sl.st. across 6 (8) [10] sts., pattern to
last 6 (8) [10] sts., 1 ch., turn.
2nd row: Work in pattern.
3rd row: Sl.st. across first 2 sts., pattern to last
2 sts., turn.
4th row: Work in pattern.
Rep. last 2 rows eight times. Fasten off.

Pocket Flaps (4 *required*)
Using No. 8 crochet hook, ch. 20 (20) [20] and
work in pattern as Back until work measures
2 (2) [2] in. Work 2 rows of d.c. round 3 sides
of flap. Fasten off.

Cuffs (2 *required*)
Using No. 8 crochet hook, ch. 42 (46) [50] and
work in pattern as Back for 2½ (2½) [2½] in.
Then work 2 rows of d.c. Fasten off.

Front Edgings
Using No. 9 crochet hook, rejoin yarn at lower
right front edge and work in d.c. up right front,
round back of neck and down left front and
round lower edges, making 7 buttonholes of
2 ch. spaces up right front, the first one 2 in.
from lower edge and the last one at commencement of neck shaping.
Next row: Work 1 d.c. into each d.c. of previous
row, working 2 d.c. into 2 ch. space.
Next row: 1 d.c. into each d.c. of previous row.
Fasten off.

Neck Band
With right side of work facing and commencing
at right neck edge, rejoin yarn and using
No. 9 crochet hook work in d.c. round to left
neck edge.
Work in d.c. for 2 in. Fasten off.

continued on page 89

Cushion and bedspread to match *Illustrated on page 6*

CUSHION
Materials:
Oddments of Lavenda Double Six. The original took 9 ozs.
20 by 20 in. material for backing.
18 in. square cushion pad.
Crochet hook No. 6 (5·00 mm).

Measurements: 18 in. square.

Tension: Each square measures 6 in.

Abbreviations:
ch. chain; tr. treble; sl.st. slip stitch
All trebles are worked into spaces not into chain. Colours for squares may be alternated but we suggest that the same shade is used for first and 4th round on each square.

THE SQUARE
Using No. 6 hook and 1st shade, ch. 5 and join into circle. This pattern is made up of blocks of 4 tr. but each round starts with 2 ch.; this counts as the first of the 4 tr., i.e. 2 ch., 3 tr., 3 ch., 4 tr., 3 ch., 4 tr., 3 ch., 4 tr. into circle, 3 ch., sl.st. into top ch. of first block (from now 4 tr. will be referred to as 1 block). Break wool.

Using 2nd shade, hook into corner space, draw wool through and make 2 ch., 1 block, 3 ch., 1 block into this space, repeat in the remaining 3 corners, join square and sl.st. to the corner space. Break wool.

Using 3rd shade work * 1 block, 3 ch:, 1 block into corner space, 1 block into centre space, repeat from * round, join square and break wool.

Using 1st shade work * 1 block, 3 ch., 1 block into corner space, 1 block into each of next 2 spaces, repeat from * round, join square and break wool.

Using 4th shade work * 1 block, 3 ch., 1 block into corner space, 1 block into next 3 spaces, repeat from * round, join square and break wool.
Work 9 squares and join together to form 18 in. square. Press back with material, leaving one side open, insert cushion pad and join remaining seam.

BEDSPREAD
Materials:
Oddments of Lavenda Double Six.
The original was worked in 4 shades, taking 47 ozs in black, 34 ozs in white, 30 ozs in brown and 28 ozs in blue.
Crochet hook No. 6 (5·00 mm).

Measurement: 72 in. by 90 in.
Tension and abbreviations as for the Cushion.
Work 180 squares as Cushion.
Join together into 15 strips of 12 squares then join each strip together. Press.

An evening bag with a glitter *Illustrated on page 44*

Materials:
1 oz. of Twilley's Goldfingering.
Aero crochet hook No. 10 (3·00 mm); 4½ in. bag frame.

Measurements:
Depth 5 in.; width along lower edge 5 in.

Abbreviations:

ch.	chain	pct.	picot
d.c.	double crochet	in.	inches
tr.	treble	sp.	space
rep.	repeat	sts.	stitches
s.s.	slip stitch	d.tr.	double treble
lp(s).	loop(s)		

Tension: 6 sts. to 1 in.
Check the tension by working a 3 in. square in the stitch pattern.

THE BAG
With No. 10 hook commence with 31 ch. to measure 5 in.
Foundation row: 1 d.c. into 2nd ch. from hook, 1d.c. into each to end, turn.
1st row: 1 d.c. into first d.c., 1 d.c. into each d.c. to end, turn. Rep. this row until work measures 8 in. from beginning. Fasten off.
Press work lightly on the wrong side with a warm iron over a damp cloth.
Fold work in half and sew to bag frame.

A skirt in motif crochet designed by Barbara Warner

The skirt is worked from the waist down.

Materials:

Mini skirt: 8 (8:9:9) balls of Twilley's Stalite No. 3 Cotton and 4 balls of Twilley's Goldfingering.

Midi skirt: 13 (13:14:14) balls of Twilley's Stalite No. 3 Cotton and 5 balls of Twilley's Goldfingering.

Maxi skirt: 16 (16:17:17) balls of Twilley's Stalite No. 3 Cotton and 5 balls of Twilley's Goldfingering.

Aero crochet hooks No. 10 (3·00 mm) and No. 12 (2·50 mm).

1 button.

Metric weight requirements:

Mini skirt: 10 (10:11:11) 50-grm balls · of Twilley's Stalite No. 3 Cotton and 5 25-grm balls of Twilley's Goldfingering.

Midi skirt: 16 (16:17:17) 50-grm balls of Twilley's Stalite No. 3 Cotton and 6 25-grm balls of Twilley's Goldfingering.

Maxi skirt: 19 (19:20:20) 50-grm balls of Twilley's Stalite No. 3 Cotton and 6 25-grm balls of Twilley's Goldfingering.

Measurements:

To fit 34 (36, 38, 40) in. hip.
Mini skirt: 22 in.; *Midi skirt:* 30 in.;
Maxi skirt: 38 in. lengths.

Tension: Each motif is 4 in. square.
Check the tension by working a 4 in. square and a motif in the stitch pattern. If the tension is tight, use a size larger hook; if loose, use a size finer hook.

Abbreviations:

ch.	chain	sp.	space
tr.	treble	patt.	pattern
d.c.	double crochet	rep.	repeat
s.s.	slip stitch	in.	inches
st.ch.	starting chain	y.r.h.	yarn round hook
inc.	increase		
dec.	decrease	cont.	continue
beg.	beginning	S.	Stalite

Figures in brackets refer to larger sizes. Where only one figure is given, this refers to all sizes.

MOTIF

Using No. 10 hook and S. make 4 ch., join into a ring with a s.s. Work 8 d.c. into ring. Fasten off. Using Goldfingering double:

2nd round: Hook into top of first d.c. and make 3 ch., * y.r.h. hook into the same d.c., y.r.h. and pull through a long loop – note this is important – y.r.h. and pull through 2 loops, rep. from * once, then y.r.h. and pull through all loops on hook, 2 ch., ** miss 1 d.c. *** y.r.h. hook into next d.c., y.r.h. and pull through a long loop, y.r.h. and pull through 2 loops, * y.r.h. hook into same d.c., y.r.h. and pull through a long loop, y.r.h. and pull through 2 loops, rep. from * once, y.r.h. and pull through all loops on hook, 2 ch., rep. from *** but work into the same d.c. as the petal just formed, then rep. from ** twice, 2 ch., then work one petal into the first d.c. of round which has one petal, 2 ch., s.s. into the top of st.ch. Fasten off.

Rejoin S. to a 2 ch. sp.

3rd round: (3 ch., standing as 1 tr., 2 tr., 2 ch., 3 tr.) into the 2 ch. sp., 3 tr. into next 2 ch. sp., * (3 tr., 2 ch., 3 tr.) into next 2 ch. sp., 3 tr. into next 2 ch. sp., rep. from * twice, then s.s. into the top of st.ch.

4th round: S.s. into 2 ch. sp., (3 ch., 2 tr., 2 ch., 3 tr.) into the 2 ch. sp., 3 tr. into sp. between next blocks of 3 tr., (3 tr., 2 ch., 3 tr.) into 2 ch. sp., in corner, rep. round, ending with a s.s. into the top of st.ch. Cont. until 4 rounds in S. are completed, working (3 tr., 2 ch., 3 tr.) into each corner sp. and 3 tr. into each sp. between blocks of 3 tr. of previous rounds. Fasten off.

PRESSING

Press each motif to the correct measurement (4 in. square).

MAKING UP

Mini skirt: Work 55 (55:60:60) motifs in all. Join 11 (11:12:12) motifs in width and 5 rows deep (or length required). Join each motif on the back with a row of d.c., leave the first 2 rows open for the centre-back opening. Work 3 rows of d.c. evenly around the hemline and finish with a row of picots. * Work 4 d.c., 4 ch., then s.s. into the first ch. of these 4 ch., rep. from * round the hem, ending with a s.s. into the top of first d.c. Fasten off.

Midi skirt: Work 77 (77:84:84) motifs in all. Join 11 (11:12:12) motifs in width and 7 rows deep. Join each motif and hem line as given for Mini skirt.

continued on page 73

A lacy duchesse set for your dressing table

Materials:
3 25-grm balls of Twilley's Lystra.
Milwards steel crochet hook No. 2 (1·75 mm).

Measurements:
10½ in. by 14 in. and 7 in. by 10½ in.

Tension: 2 motifs to 7 in.
Check the tension by working and joining 2 motifs. If the tension is tight use a size larger hook, if loose use a size finer hook.

Abbreviations:

ch.	chain	s.s.	slip stitch
d.c.	double crochet	dbl.tr.	double treble
hlf.tr.	half treble	rep.	repeat
tr.	treble	pct.	picot
lp(s).	loop(s)	sp.	space

1st MOTIF
6 ch., s.s. into first ch. to form a ring.
1st round: (1 d.c. into ring 5 ch.) 6 times, s.s. into 1st d.c. (6 sp.).
2nd round: Into each lp. make 1 d.c., 1 hlf.tr., 5 tr., 1 hlf.tr., 1 d.c., end with s.s. into 1st d.c.
3rd round: * 5 ch., insert hook through 2 lps. of next d.c. on 1st round at back of work, rep. from * s.s. into 1st d.c.
4th round: In each lp. work 1 d.c., 1 hlf.tr., 7 tr., 1 hlf.tr., 1 d.c., end with s.s. into 1st d.c.
5th round: S.s. into each of first 3 sts. of next petal, 1 d.c. into next sp. * 5 ch., s.s. into 3rd ch. from hook (a pct. made), 3 ch., 1 pct., 2 ch., miss 3 sts., s.s. into next st., 2 ch., 1 pct.,

3 ch., 1 pct., 2 ch., miss 3 sts. of next petal, 1 d.c. into next st., rep. from * all round, s.s. into 1st d.c.
6th round: S.s. across to first 3 ch. following next pct., s.s. into lp., 4 ch., leaving last lp. of each dbl.tr. on hook make 3 dbl.tr. into same lp., yarn over hook and draw through all lps. on hook (a cluster made), 3 ch., 1 pct., 5 ch., 1 pct., 3 ch., make a 4 dbl.tr. cluster into same lp., into each lp. make a cluster, 3 ch., 1 pct., 5 ch., 1 pct., 3 ch., a cluster; end with s.s. into top of first cluster. Fasten off.

2nd MOTIF
Work as for first motif until 5th round is completed.
6th round: Complete 1st cluster, (3 ch., 1 pct., 2 ch., 1 s.s. into corresponding lp. of first motif, 2 ch., 1 pct., 3 ch., a cluster into same place as last cluster on 2nd motif, a cluster into next lp.) twice, complete as for 1st motif. Make a doily 3 motifs by 4, and 2 small doilys 2 motifs by 3, joining motifs as 2nd motif was joined to 1st motif, leaving one lp. free on each motif between joinings.

Fill-in-lace: Commence with 10 ch., s.s. into first ch. to form a ring.
1st round: 16 d.c. into ring, s.s. into 1st d.c.
2nd round: * 2 ch. 1 pct., 2 ch., s.s. into free lp. between joinings, 2 ch., 1 pct., 2 ch., miss 3 d.c. on ring, 1 d.c. into next d.c., 10 ch., s.s. into joining 10 ch., s.s. into same place as last d.c. on ring, rep. from * all round, s.s. into 1st d.c. Fasten off. Starch and press.

Collar and cuff set *Illustrated on page 27*

Materials:
2 ozs Twilley's Goldfingering or Lyscordet.
Stratnoid crochet hook No. 9 (3·50 mm).

Measurements (*adjustable*):
Length at neck edge of collar 15 in.
Cuff length 7½ in.

Tension:
7 tr. to 1 in. measured over plain tr.
Check the tension by working a 4 in. square in treble. If the tension is tight use a larger size hook; if loose use a size finer hook.

Abbreviations:

ch.	chain	sts.	stitches
tr.	treble	s.s.	slip stitch
d.c.	double crochet	rep.	repeat
sp.	space	y.o.h.	yarn over hook
lp(s).	loop(s)	in.	inch

Instructions are given for cuffs. Figures in brackets refer to collar. Where only one figure is given this refers to both.

Commence with 54 (110) ch. to measure 7¾ (15¼) in.; adjust length here by working an additional 8 ch. for every extra 1⅛ in. required.
Foundation row: 1 d.c. into 2nd ch. from hook, 1 d.c. into each ch. to end, turn.
1st row: 5 ch., miss first 2 d.c., 1 tr. into next d.c., * 2 ch., miss next d.c., 1 tr. into next d.c., rep. from * to end. 26 (54) sp., turn.
2nd row: 1 d.c. into first tr., * 2 d.c. into next sp., 1 d.c. into next tr., rep. from * 2 d.c. into next sp., 1 d.c. into 3rd of 5 ch., turn.
3rd row: 5 ch., miss first 3 d.c., y.o.h., insert hook into next d.c. and draw a lp. up, (y.o.h., insert hook into same place, draw a lp. up) 4 times, y.o.h. and draw through all lps. on hook (a puff st. formed), 3 ch., a puff st. into same place, * 4 ch., miss 5 d.c., 1 d.c. into next d.c., 4 ch., miss 5 d.c., a puff st. into next d.c., 3 ch., a puff st. into same d.c., rep. from * 2 ch., miss 2 d.c., 1 tr. into last d.c., turn.
4th row: 5 ch., * into next 3 ch. sp. work (a puff st., 3 ch.) twice, a puff st. into same sp., 4 ch., 1 d.c. into next d.c., 4 ch., rep. from *, into last 3 ch. sp. work (a puff st., 3 ch.) twice, a puff st. into same sp., 2 ch., 1 tr. into 3rd of 5 ch., turn.
5th row: 3 ch., * into each of next 2, 3 ch. sp. work (a puff st., 3 ch.) twice, 4 ch., 1 d.c. into next d.c., 4 ch., rep. from *, into next 3 ch. sp. work (a puff st., 3 ch.) twice, into last 3 ch. sp. work a puff st., 3 ch., a puff st., 1 tr. into 3rd of 5 ch. Fasten off.

Edging
With right side facing attach yarn to row-end of foundation row, 1 d.c. into same place, *** 2 d.c. into next sp., 3 ch., 1 s.s. into top of last d.c., rep. from * until a 4 ch. sp. is reached, 3 d.c. into each of next 2 sps., 3 ch., s.s. into top of last d.c., rep. from ** then work *** 2 d.c. into next sp., 3 ch., s.s. into top of last d.c., rep. from *** 1 d.c. into row-end of foundation row. Fasten off.

Skirts *continued from page 71*

Maxi skirt: Work 99 (99:108:108) motifs in all. Join 11 (11:12:12) motifs in width and 9 rows deep. Join each motif and hem line as given for Mini skirt.

WAISTBAND
Using No. 12 hook and S. starting from centre back work 10 (10:9:9) d.c. evenly into each square (this is to draw the waist in). Work 8 rows in d.c. Fasten off. Sew button on to waistband and make a loop chain on opposite side for buttonhole.

Press skirt lightly on the wrong side with a warm iron over a damp cloth.

TABS
Using No. 10 hook make 9 ch., and working into the 2nd ch. from hook, work 1 d.c. into each ch. turn. Work 4 rows in d.c. Fasten off. Make 8 tabs and sew these at regular intervals along the waistband. Thread ribbon or a belt through the tabs.

See page 94 for washing instructions. Do not use enzyme washing powders.

A luxurious bed-jacket

Threaded with ribbon, this charming bed-jacket is easy and quick to make. Use a colour of your own choice with contrasting ribbon.

Materials:

Lister Bel Air Crochet Yarn	15 balls
Lister Bri-nylon Double Knitting	15 balls
Lavenda Double Knitting	15 ozs

No. 7 (4·50 mm) crochet hook
4 buttons; 3 yds ribbon

Measurements:
To fit 34–38 in. bust.
Length from shoulder 20 in.
Length of undersleeve seam 10 in.

Tension:
4 tr. to 1 in.
Check tension before proceeding to work the garment.

Abbreviations:

ch. chain	tr. treble
d.c. double crochet	d.tr. double treble

YOKE
Using No. 7 crochet hook, ch. 81.
1st row: 1 tr. into 3rd ch. from hook, 1 tr. into each remaining ch. (80 tr.).
2nd row: 3 ch. (counts as 1 tr.), miss 1 tr., 1 tr. into each of next 4 tr., * 2 tr. into next tr., 1 tr. into each of next 4 tr., repeat from * to last 5 tr., 2 tr. into next tr., 1 tr. into each remaining tr. (95 tr.).
3rd and each alternate row: 3 ch. (counts as 1 tr.), miss 1 tr., 1 tr. into each tr. to end.
4th row: 3 ch., miss 1 tr., 1 tr. into each of next 4 tr., * 2 tr. into next tr., 1 tr. into each of next 5 tr., repeat from * to last 6 tr., 2 tr. into next tr., 1 tr. into each remaining tr. (110 tr.).
6th row: 3 ch., miss 1 tr., 1 tr. into each of next 5 tr., * 2 tr. into next tr., 1 tr. into each of next 6 tr., repeat from * to last 6 tr., 2 tr. into next tr., 1 tr. into each remaining tr. (125 tr.).
8th row: 3 ch., miss 1 tr., 1 tr. into each of next 6 tr., * 2 tr. into next tr., 1 tr. into each of next 7 tr., repeat from * to last 6 tr., 2 tr. into next tr., 1 tr. into each remaining tr. (140 tr.).
10th row: 3 ch., miss 1 tr., 1 tr. into each of next 7 tr., * 2 tr. into next tr., 1 tr. into each of next 8 tr., repeat from * to last 6 tr., 2 tr. into next tr., 1 tr. into each remaining tr. (155 tr.).
12th row: 3 ch., miss 1 tr., 1 tr. into each of next 8 tr., * 2 tr. into next tr., 1 tr. into each of next 9 tr., repeat from * to last 6 tr., 2 tr. into next tr., 1 tr. into each remaining tr. (170 tr.).
14th row: 3 ch., miss 1 tr., 1 tr. into each of next 9 tr., * 2 tr. into next tr., 1 tr. into each of next 10 tr., repeat from * to last 6 tr., 2 tr. into next tr., 1 tr. into each of next 4 tr., 2 tr. into end tr. (186 tr.).
15th row: 4 ch., miss 2 tr., 3 d.tr. into next tr., 1 ch., 3 d.tr. into next tr., miss 1 tr., 1 d.tr. into next tr., * 1 d.tr. into next tr., miss 1 tr., 3 d.tr. into next tr., 1 ch., 3 d.tr. into next tr., miss 1 tr., 1 d.tr. into next tr., repeat from * to end.

16th row: 4 ch., miss 4 d.tr., 3 d.tr., 1 ch., 3 d.tr. into next 1 ch. space, miss 3 d.tr., 1 d.tr. into next d.tr., * 1 d.tr. into next d.tr., miss 3 d.tr., 3 d.tr., 1 ch., 3 d.tr. into next 1 ch. space, miss 3 d.tr., 1 d.tr. into next d.tr., repeat from * to end. (31 patterns).
Repeat last row four times more.
Next row: Work in pattern across 4 patterns, miss 7 patterns, pattern across 9 patterns, miss 7 patterns, pattern across remaining 4 patterns. (17 patterns worked).
Continue in pattern on these 17 patterns until work measures 20 in. from shoulder. Fasten off.

SLEEVES
With right side facing, rejoin yarn (wool) at underarm and work in pattern across 7 patterns left for sleeve, turn, work back in pattern. Continue in pattern until sleeve measures 10 in. Fasten off.

RIGHT FRONT BAND
Commencing at lower edge of Right Front, rejoin yarn (wool) and work 2 rows in d.c.
3rd row: (Make buttonhole): Work in d.c. as far as Yoke, now make 4 buttonholes at regular intervals to neckline (to make buttonhole work 3 ch., miss 2 d.c.).
4th row: Work in d.c. working 2 d.c. into each 2 ch. space of previous row.
5th row: Work in d.c. Fasten off.

LEFT FRONT BAND
Work as Right Front Band commencing at neck edge with right side facing and omitting buttonholes.

NECK BAND
With right side facing, rejoin yarn (wool) and work 2 rows in d.c.
Next row: 3 ch., * miss 2 d.c., 1 tr. into next d.c., repeat from * to end.
Next row: 3 ch., * 5 d.tr. into next space, repeat from * to end.
Next row: 1 ch., * 1 d.c. into next d.tr., repeat from * to end. Fasten off.

TO MAKE UP
Pin out and press on wrong side using a damp cloth. Join sleeve seams. Thread ribbon through first row of d.tr. after Yoke. Thread ribbon through holes at Neck, leaving ends to tie. Add buttons to correspond with buttonholes. Press sleeve seams.

See page 94 for washing instructions.

**Gloves
for him and her**

LADIES' GLOVES
Materials:
2 ozs Twilley's Lyscordet fine knitting cotton.
Stratnoid crochet hook No. 12 (2·50 mm).
2 small buttons.

Measurements: To fit an average hand.

Tension: 7 sts. to 1 in.
Check the tension by working a 4 in. square in
the pattern. If the tension is tight use a size
larger hook, if loose use a size finer hook.

Abbreviations:

ch.	chain	rep.	repeat
tr.	treble	patt.	pattern
d.c.	double crochet	lp(s).	loop(s)
sp.	space	sl.st.	slip stitch

Right hand thumb: Wind thread round finger
to form a ring.
1st round: 9 d.c. into ring, draw commencing
ring tight.
2nd round: 2 ch., (1 tr. into next d.c., 1 ch.) 8
times, 1 d.c. into 2 ch. lp.
Patt. round: Working in continuous rounds
make * 1 ch., 1 d.c. into next tr.; rep. from *
until 7 rounds have been formed ** (1 ch.,
1 d.c. into next sp.) twice, fasten off.
3rd finger: Work as for thumb but working
patt. round until 9 rounds have been completed,
end as for thumb.

2nd and 4th fingers: Work as for thumb but
working patt. round until 8 rounds have been
completed, end as for thumb.
1st finger: Work as for thumb until ** is
reached. Do not fasten off.

RIGHT HAND
1st round: 1 ch., 1 tr. into next sp., * 1 ch.,
leaving last lp. of each tr. on hook make 1 tr.
into next sp. on 1st finger, 1 tr. into first sp.
formed on 2nd finger, thread over hook and
draw through all lps. on hook (a cluster
formed), (1 ch., 1 tr. into next sp. on 2nd finger)
twice; rep. from * across 3rd and 4th fingers
respectively, (1 ch., 1 tr. into next sp.) 4 times
on 4th finger, a cluster into last sp. on 4th
finger and next sp. on 3rd finger, (1 ch., 1 tr.
into next sp. on 3rd finger) twice; rep. from
* across 2nd and 1st fingers respectively, 1 ch.,
1 tr. into next sp.
Work patt. round 4 times.

Thumb insert and Back opening
Next round: Lay work down flat with palm
facing upwards, mark sp. on last round at
centre back and at 4th finger edge, ** work
patt. round to within 3 sps. before marked sp.
on 4th finger edge, 1 ch., a cluster into next sp.
and into 1st sp. on thumb, (1 ch., 1 tr. into next sp.)
1 tr. into next sp.) 4 times on thumb, 1 ch., a
cluster into next sp. on thumb and into marked
sp. on main part, * 1 ch., 1 tr. into next sp.;

rep. from * to within 2 sp. before marked sp. at centre back, turn. **

1st row: 3 ch., * 1 tr. into next sp., 1 ch.; rep. from * to within 3 sp. before marked sp., 1 tr. into next tr., turn.

2nd row: 3 ch., * 1 tr. into next sp., 1 ch.; rep. from * ending with 1 tr. into 3rd of 3 ch., turn.

Rep. last row 4 times more.

Edging

1st row: 10 ch., 1 d.c. into 2nd ch. from hook, 3 ch., miss 3 ch., 1 d.c. into each ch., 1 d.c. into each sp. along top of glove, 3 d.c. into corner, then work d.c. evenly round back opening, 1 d.c. into 1st corner d.c., turn.

2nd row: 1 d.c. into first d.c., 1 d.c. into each d.c., 3 d.c. into corner, 1 d.c. into each st. along top of glove, turn.

3rd row: 1 d.c. into first d.c., 1 d.c. into each d.c. along top of glove until corner is reached, fasten off.

LEFT HAND

Work as for right hand until thumb insert is reached.

Thumb insert and Back opening

Lay work down flat with palm facing upwards and mark sp. on last round at centre back and at 4th finger edge, work patt. round to within 2 sp. before sp. at centre back, turn.

Next row: 3 ch., * 1 tr. into next sp., then work from ** to ** of right hand.

Work 2nd row of right hand 5 times.

Edging

1st row: 1 d.c. into first tr., 1 d.c. into each sp. on top of glove, 10 ch., 1 d.c. into 2nd ch. from hook, 3 ch., miss 3 ch., 1 d.c. into each ch., then work d.c. evenly round back opening, 2 d.c. into corner, 1 sl.st. into 1st d.c., turn.

Work 2nd and 3rd rows of right hand, fasten off.

Finishing: Sew up gaps between fingers and thumb, then sew buttons into position to correspond with buttonholes. Press lightly.

MEN'S GLOVES

Materials:

5 ozs. Twilley's Lyscordet knitting cotton No. 3. Stratnoid crochet hook No. 10 (3·00 mm). 2 small buttons.

Measurements: To fit an average hand.

Tension: 6 sts. to 1 in.

Work as for ladies' gloves.

Dresses *continued from page 64*

3rd row: (1 tr., 1 ch., 1 tr.) in centre of first bell, 1 tr. in sp. between first and 2nd bell, * (1 tr., 1 ch., 1 tr.) in centre of next bell, 1 tr. in sp. between this bell and next bell, rep. from * 3 (3; 3; 4; 4; 5) times, (1 tr., 1 ch., 1 tr.) in 1st tr. of 13 (13; 13; 16; 19; 19) tr. of previous row, ** miss 1 tr., 1 tr. in next tr., miss 1 tr., (1 tr., 1 ch., 1 tr.) in next tr., rep. from ** 2 (2; 2; 3; 4; 4) times, making 3·(3; 3; 4; 5; 5) (1 tr., 1 ch., 1 tr.) blocks, *** (1 tr., 1 ch., 1 tr.) in centre of next bell, 1 tr. in sp. between this and next bell, rep. from *** to second set of 13 (13; 13; 16; 19; 19) tr., working across these in same manner as before, **** (1 tr., 1 ch., 1 tr.) in centre of next bell, 1 tr. in sp. between this and next bell, rep. from **** to end, working 1 tr. in end tr., 3 ch., turn.

4th row: 1 bell in centre of first (1 tr., 1 ch., 1 tr.) block, * 1 bell in next (1 tr., 1 ch., 1 tr.) block, rep. from * to end, working 1 tr. in end tr., 3 ch., turn.

5th row: (1 tr., 1 ch., 1 tr.) in centre of 1st bell, * 1 tr. in sp. between 1st and 2nd bell, (1 tr., 1 ch., 1 tr.) in centre of next bell, rep. from * to end, working 1 tr. in end tr., 3 ch., turn.

The 4th and 5th rows form the patt. throughout. Cont. in patt. until work measures 15 (17; 20; 30; 32; 34) in. from comm. or one inch shorter than desired length, ending after a 5th patt. row.

Next row: (2 L.T., 3 ch., 1 sl.st. in 3rd ch. from hook, 2 L.T.) all into centre of first (1 tr., 1 ch., 1 tr.) sp., * (2 L.T., 3 ch., 1 sl.st. in 3rd ch. from hook, 2 L.T.) all into centre of next (1 tr., 1 ch., 1 tr.) sp., rep. from * to end, working 1 tr. in end tr. Fasten off.

TO COMPLETE

Using a damp cloth and warm iron, press lightly. Sew up back seam to 1½ (1½; 1½; 2; 2; 2) in. below yoke. Press seam. Sew in zip to close yoke. For washing instructions, see page 94.

For Lorette: If pressing is desired use a dry cloth and a cool iron. Press lightly.

Children's sweaters

Materials:
For chest sizes: 26 28 30 in.
Lee Target Motoravia
   Double Knitting Wool 11 12 13 ozs
Lee Target Lorette
   Double Crepe 11 12 13 balls
Lee Target Super Crimp
   Bri-nylon Double
   Knitting 11 12 13 balls
Crochet hooks Nos. 8 (4·00 mm) and
   9 (3·50 mm)

Measurements:
For chest sizes: 26 28 30 in.
Length from top of
   shoulder 16 17½ 19 in.
Sleeve seam 11 12 13 in.

Tension:
4 tr. to 1 in. and 5 rows to 2 in. deep, using
No. 8 hook.

Abbreviations:
ch. chain   tr. treble
d.c. double crochet st. stitch
d.tr. double treble   sl. slip
C4tr.B – Miss next 2 tr., 1 tr. in each of next

2 tr., 1 tr. in each of 2 missed tr., working with
wool (yarn) and hook round back of 2 tr. just
worked.
C4tr.F – Miss next 2 tr., 1 tr. in each of next
2 tr., 1 tr. in each of 2 missed tr., working with
wool (yarn) and hook across front of 2 tr. just
worked.
Dec. 1 – Work next 2 tr. leaving last loop on
hook each time, wool (yarn) over hook draw
through 3 loops together, thus decreasing one
stitch.

Follow first set of figures given for 26 in. size.
Follow first set of figures in brackets for 28 in.
size.
Follow second set of figures in brackets for 30
in. size.

BACK
Using No. 9 hook make 61 (65; 69) ch.
1st row: 1 d.c. in 2nd ch. from hook, 1 d.c. in
each remaining ch. 60 (64; 68) d.c.
2nd row: 1 d.c. in each d.c.
Repeat 2nd row 4 times, 2 ch. turn after last
row.
2 ch. counts as first tr. on every row.
Using No. 8 hook, proceed as follows:

1st row: (1 tr. in next d.c.) 21 (23; 25) times, (C4tr.B, C4tr.F) twice, (1 tr. in next d.c.) 22 (24; 26) times, 2 ch., turn.
2nd row: 1 tr. in each tr. to end, 2 ch., turn.
3rd row: (1 tr. in next tr.) 21 (23; 25) times, (C4tr.F, C4tr.B) twice, (1 tr. in next tr.) 22 (24; 26) times, 2 ch., turn.
4th row: As 2nd row.
These 4 rows form the pattern.
Continue in pattern until work measures 10 (11; 12) in., ending with a 2nd row (omitting 2 ch. turn after last row).

Shape raglan (Right side facing)
1st row: Sl.st. over 5 tr., pattern to last 5 tr., 2 ch., turn.
2nd row: 1 tr. in next tr., dec. 1, pattern to last 4 tr., dec. 1, 1 tr. in each of next 2 tr., 2 ch., turn.
Repeat 2nd row until 20 (22; 24) tr. remain. Fasten off.

FRONT
Work exactly as Back until raglan shapings are reached.
Shape raglan
1st row: Sl.st. over 5 tr., pattern to last 5 tr., 2 ch., turn.
2nd row: 1 tr. in next tr., dec. 1, pattern to last 4 tr., dec. 1, 1 tr. in each of next 2 tr., 2 ch., turn.

Shape neck
1st row: 1 tr. in next tr., dec. 1, pattern 12 (14; 16) tr., C4tr.B, 1 tr. in each of next 4 tr., 2 ch., turn. Leave remaining 24 (26; 28) tr. for other side.
2nd row: Dec. 1, pattern to last 4 tr., dec. 1, 1 tr. in each of next 2 tr., 2 ch., turn.
3rd row: 1 tr. in next tr., dec. 1, pattern to last 3 tr., dec. 1, 1 tr. in end tr., 2 ch., turn.
Repeat 2nd and 3rd rows 0 (0; 1) times.
Next row: Pattern to last 4 tr., dec. 1, 1 tr. in each of next 2 tr., 2 ch., turn.
Next row: As 3rd row.
Repeat last 2 rows until 6 sts. remain.
Next row: (Dec. 1) twice, 1 tr. in end tr., 2 ch., turn.
Next row: Dec. 1. 1 tr. in end tr. Fasten off.

Return to neck shaping, rejoin wool (yarn) to next tr.
1st row: 1 tr. in each of 4 tr., C4tr.F, pattern 12 (14; 16) tr., dec. 1, 1 tr. in each of next 2 tr., 2 ch., turn.
2nd row: 1 tr. in next tr., dec. 1, pattern to last 3 tr., dec. 1, 1 tr. in end tr., 2 ch., turn.

3rd row: Dec. 1, pattern to last 4 tr., dec. 1, 1 tr. in each of next 2 tr., 2 ch., turn.
Repeat 2nd and 3rd rows 0 (0; 1) times.
Next row: 1 tr. in next tr., dec. 1, pattern to end.
Next row: As 3rd row.
Repeat last 2 rows until 6 sts. remain.
Next row: (Dec. 1) twice, 1 tr. in end tr., 2 ch., turn.
Next row: Dec. 1, 1 tr. in end tr. Fasten off.

SLEEVES
Using No. 9 hook make 27 (27; 27) ch.
1st row: 1 d.c. in 2nd ch. from hook. 26 (26; 26) d.c.
2nd row: 1 d.c. in each d.c.
Repeat 2nd row 10 times, 2 ch., turn after last row.
Using No. 8 hook, proceed as follows:
1st row: 1 tr. in each d.c., 2 ch., turn.
2nd row: 1 tr. in each tr., 2 ch., turn.
The 2nd row forms the pattern for the Sleeve.
Continue in pattern, increasing 1 tr. at each end of next and every following alternate row until there are 44 (46; 48) tr.
Continue without shaping until work measures 11 (12; 13) in. or desired length of sleeve seam.

Shape raglan
As Back until 4 tr. remain. Fasten off.

TO MAKE UP
Press each piece carefully using a damp cloth and warm iron. Sew in sleeves. Sew up side and sleeve seams.

NECKBAND
Using No. 9 hook, commencing at Left Back Raglan, rejoin wool (yarn).
1st round: Work 4 d.c. across top of sleeve; 28 (30; 32) d.c. down Left Front, 28 (30; 32) d.c. up Right Front; 4 d.c. across top of sleeve; 18 (20; 22) d.c. across Back, sl.st. to complete round, turn.
2nd round: (1 d.c. in next d.c.) 48 (52; 56) times, miss next 3 d.c., 1 d.c. in each d.c. to end. Sl.st. to complete round, turn.
3rd round: (1 d.c. in next d.c.) 29 (31; 33) times, miss next 3 d.c., 1 d.c. in each d.c. to end, sl.st. to complete round. Fasten off.
Press all seams.

See page 94 for washing instructions. *For Lorette:* dry away from direct heat, and if pressing is desired use a cool iron over a dry cloth. Press lightly.

Sleeveless coat *Illustrated on page 47*

Materials:

Lister Lavenda Double Knitting	17 ozs.
Lister Bri-Nylon Double Knitting	17 balls
Lister Bel Air Double Crepe	8 balls

Crochet hook Nos. 8 (4·00 mm) and
9 (3·50 mm)

Measurements:
To fit 32–36 in. bust measurement.
Length from shoulder 32 in.

Tension:
3 tr. and 3 sp. to one inch (No. 9 or No. 8 hook).

Abbreviations: see page 60

N.B. When using Bri-Nylon Double Knitting use No. 7 (4·50 mm) hook instead of No. 8 (4·00 mm) hook and No. 8 (4·00 mm) hook instead of No. 9 (3·50 mm) hook.

MOTIF ONE (6 in. square) 12 required
Using No. 9 hook, make 17 ch.
1st row: 1 tr. in 5th ch. from hook, * 1 ch., miss 1 ch., 1 tr. in next ch., rep. from * to end. 7 ch. sp.
2nd row: 3 ch. (representing 1st tr.), miss first tr., 1 tr. in next tr., * 1 ch., miss 1 ch., 1 tr. in next tr., rep. from * to end.

Repeat 2nd row 5 times. Do not turn.
The motif is now worked in rounds. The spaces between rows and the spaces between tr. are referred to as ch. sp.

1st round: 1 ch., * 2 d.c. in each of first 3 sp. (1 d.c., 4 ch., 1 d.c.) in next sp., 2 d.c. in each of next 3 sp. to corner, 1 ch., rep. from * along remaining 3 sides.

2nd round: 1 d.c. in first ch. of previous round, * 6 sl.st. across 6 d.c., [1 d.c. in 4 ch. sp., 3 ch., 1 sl.st. in first of these 3 ch. (pic. made)] 5 times, 1 d.c. in 4 ch. sp., 6 sl.st. across 6 d.c. to corner ch., 1 d.c. in this ch., rep. from * on remaining 3 sides omitting last d.c.

3rd round: * 1 d.c. in corner d.c., 5 ch., 1 sl.st. into top of 2nd pic., 6 ch., 1 sl.st. in top of 4th pic., 5 ch., rep. from * along remaining 3 sides.

4th round: * 1 d.c. in corner d.c., 5 d.c. in 5 ch. sp., 1 d.c. in sl.st. (4 d.c., 2 ch., 4 d.c.) in 6 ch. sp., 1 d.c. in next sl.st., 5 d.c. in 5 ch. sp., rep. from * along remaining 3 sides, 1 sl.st. in first d.c.

5th round: 1 d.c. in each of 10 d.c. to 2 ch. sp., * 1 d.c., 2 ch., 1 d.c. in this sp., 19 d.c. to next 2 ch. sp., rep. from * on next 2 sides, 1 d.c., 2 ch., 1 d.c. in 2 ch. sp., 9 d.c. to end of round. Fasten off with sl.st. on first d.c.

6th round: Rejoin yarn to corner ch. sp. with 4 ch. (representing 1 tr., 1 ch.), miss 1 d.c., 1 tr. in next d.c., (1 ch., miss 1 d.c., 1 tr. in next d.c.) 9 times, * 1 ch., (1 tr., 1 ch., 1 tr.) in corner ch. sp., (1 ch., miss 1 d.c., 1 tr. in next d.c.) 10 times, rep. from * twice, 1 ch., 1 tr. in same place as first 4 ch., 1 ch., 1 sl.st. into 3rd of these ch.

7th round: * 1 d.c. in first ch. sp., 1 d.c. in next tr., rep. from * to corner ch. sp., 1 d.c. in this sp., 1 d.c. in next tr. ** Rep. from * to ** on remaining 3 sides. Fasten off with sl.st. on first d.c.

MOTIF TWO (6¼ in. square) 6 required
Work exactly as given for No. 1 motif until round 5 has been worked. Work rounds 6 and 7 using No. 8 hook.

MOTIF THREE (6½ in. square) 6 required
Work exactly as given for No. 1 motif until round 4 has been worked. Work rounds 5, 6 and 7 using No. 8 hook.

MOTIF FOUR (5½ in. square) 4 required
Work exactly as given for No. 1 motif until round 4 has been worked. Fasten off with sl.st. on first d.c.

The 3 rows edging is now worked on 2 sides of motif only, using No. 9 hook as follows:
Rejoin yarn to corner 2 ch. sp. with 1 d.c.

1st row: 1 d.c. in each of 19 d.c. to next 2 ch. sp., 1 d.c., 2 ch., 1 d.c. in this sp., 19 d.c. to next corner sp., 4 ch., turn.

2nd row: * Miss first d.c., (1 tr. in next d.c., 1 ch., miss 1 d.c.) 10 times, * (1 tr., 1 ch., 1 tr., 1 ch.) in 2 ch. sp., rep. from * to *, 1 tr. in end d.c., turn.

3rd row: 1 d.c. in first tr., * 1 d.c. in ch. sp., 1 d.c. in next tr., rep. from * to end. Fasten off.

MOTIF FIVE (4 required)
Using No. 9 hook, make 15 ch.

1st row: Miss first ch., 1 d.c. in each of next 6 ch., 1 d.c. in next ch., 4 ch., 1 d.c. in next ch., 1 d.c. in each d.c. to end, 1 ch., turn.

2nd row: 6 sl.st. across 6 d.c. to 4 ch. sp., 5 pic. in this sp., 6 sl.st. across 6 d.c. to end, 1 ch., turn.

3rd row: 1 d.c. in first sl.st., 5 ch., 1 sl.st. in 2nd pic., 6 ch., 1 sl.st. on 4th pic., 5 ch., 1 d.c. in end ch.

4th row: 1 d.c. in first d.c., 5 d.c. in 5 ch. sp., 1 d.c. in next sl.st. (4 d.c., 2 ch., 4 d.c.) in 6 ch. sp., 1 d.c. in next sl.st., 5 d.c. in 5 ch. sp., 1 d.c. in end d.c. Fasten off.

Press each motif carefully, using a damp cloth and warm iron. Sew together as shown in diagram, placing one tr. border of two No. 4 motifs to two No. 1 motifs at centre back and remaining tr. borders together at centre back. Place one tr. border of each No. 4 motif at fronts to centre front and sew remaining tr. borders to motif 1. Sew edges of two No. 5 motifs together to form shoulder seams. Press all seams.

YOKE
With right side facing, using No. 9 hook, commence at Right front, rejoin yarn with 1 ch. to corner of neck, 1 tr. at base of first tr., 1 ch., 1 tr. in first d.c. (1 ch., miss 1 d.c., 1 tr. in next d.c.) 4 times, 1 ch., 1 tr. in sp. between 3rd and 4th rows of Front Motif No. 5, 1 ch., 1 tr. in corner, (1 ch., miss 1 ch., 1 tr. in next ch.) 14 times, 1 ch., miss 1 ch., 1 tr. in corner, 1 ch., 1 tr. between 3rd and 4th rows of Back Motif No. 5, 1 ch., 1 tr. in joining seam, working across back neck, (1 ch., miss 1 d.c., 1 tr. in next d.c.) 5 times, 1 ch., 1 tr. in tr. sp., 1 ch.,

1 tr. in joining seam, 1 ch., 1 tr. in tr. sp., (1 ch., miss 1 d.c., 1 tr. in next d.c.) 5 times, 1 ch., 1 tr. in joining seam, 1 ch., 1 tr. between 3rd and 4th rows of Back Motif No. 5, 1 ch., 1 tr. in corner, (1 ch., miss 1 d.c., 1 tr. in next d.c.) 15 times, 1 ch., 1 tr. between 3rd and 4th rows of Front Motif No. 5, (1 ch., miss 1 d.c., 1 tr. in next d.c.) 5 times, 1 ch., 1 tr. at base of first tr. at front edge, 1 ch., 1 sl.st. in corner, 3 ch., turn.

2nd row: * 1 d.c. in first ch. sp., 1 d.c. in next tr., * rep. to * to 15 tr. across back neck, (1 tr. in next tr., 1 ch., miss 1 ch. sp.) 15 times, rep. from * to * to front edge, 3 ch., turn.

3rd row: * Miss 2 d.c., 1 tr. in next d.c., 1 ch., * rep. from * to 15 tr. at back neck, (1 tr. in next tr., 1 ch.) 15 times, rep. from * to * to end, omitting last ch. [48 tr. sp.].

4th row: 1 d.c. in first tr., (1 d.c. in tr. sp., 1 d.c. in next tr.) 12 times, (1 d.c. in tr. sp., 1 d.c. in each of next 2 tr.) 12 times, (1 d.c. in tr. sp., 1 d.c. in next tr.) 12 times. Fasten off.

FRONT BORDERS
AND NECK EDGING
Using No. 9 hook.
With right side facing, rejoin yarn to lower edge of Right Front, work d.c. evenly up front edge and around neck working 2 d.c. in each corner d.c. of neck, then down left side to lower edge. Work 4 more rows, working 3 buttonholes evenly spaced between neck edge and first motif on 1st and 2nd row as follows:

TO MAKE BUTTONHOLE
1st row: D.c. to buttonhole position, 2 ch., miss 2 d.c., d.c. to next position.
2nd row: Work in d.c. to 2 ch., 2 d.c. in 2 ch. sp.

ARMHOLE EDGING
With right side facing, using No. 9 hook, commence at base of left side of armhole, work d.c. evenly around armhole, then work 1 d.c. in each d.c. across motif at underarm.
2nd round: 3 ch., miss 1 d.c., * 1 tr. in next d.c., 1 ch., miss 1 d.c., repeat from * to underarm motif.
Across top of underarm motif work as follows: 1 tr. in next d.c., 1 ch., miss 2 d.c., join with sl.st. to top of first 3 ch.
3rd round: * 1 d.c. in ch. sp., 1 d.c. in next tr., rep. from * to end. Fasten off with sl.st. in first d.c. Press carefully. Sew on buttons to correspond with buttonholes.

How to make up the coat. The numbers refer to the motif numbers.

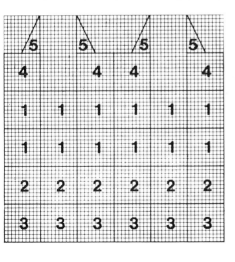

A dream of a dress

Lucky the bride who crochets this charming dress for the greatest day in her life. The dress and bolero are simple and quick to make, and will do duty for evening wear as well.

Measurements:

Bust	34	36	38	in.
Hips	36	38	40	in.
Dress length	52½	53	53½	in.
Bolero	10½	11	11½	in.
Sleeve seam	3¼	3¼	3¼	in.

Materials:

Dress

Crysette	27	28	31	balls
Stalite	14	14	16	balls
Goldfingering	3	4	4	balls

A 14 in. zip fastener
2½ yds (2·29 m) lining material, 36 in. (91·4 cm) wide Hook and eye.

Bolero

Crysette	8	9	10	balls
Stalite	4	5	5	balls
Goldfingering	1	1	1	ball

1 small button

Aero crochet hooks No. 9 (3·50 mm) and
                        No. 10 (3·00 mm).

Metric weight requirements:

Dress

Crysette	30	31	34	25 grm balls
Stalite	16	16	18	50 grm balls
Goldfingering	4	5	6	25 grm balls

Bolero

Crysette	9	10	11	25 grm balls
Stalite	5	6	6	50 grm balls
Goldfingering	2	2	2	25 grm balls

Tension:

6 sts. and 7 rows to 1 in. over d.c., using No. 10 hook.

Check the tension by working a 4 in. square in the stitch pattern. If the tension is tight, use a size larger hook, if loose, use a size finer hook.

Abbreviations:

ch.	chain	inc.	increase
d.c.	double crochet	sp.	space
sts.	stitches	s.s.	slip stitch
in.	inches	tr.	treble
dec.	decrease		

Figures in brackets refer to larger sizes. Where only one figure is given this refers to all sizes.

FRONT BODICE

Using No. 10 hook commence with 88 (94:100) ch.

1st row: 1 d.c. into 2nd ch. from hook, 1 d.c. into each ch. to end, 1 ch., turn.

The turning ch. at end of rows represents the first d.c. of following rows, the last d.c. of rows is worked into the turning ch. of previous row. Work through both loops of sts. throughout.

2nd and 3rd rows: 1 d.c. into each d.c. to end, 1 ch., turn.

To shape for dart

4th row: 1 d.c. into each of next 34 d.c., 2 d.c. into next d.c., 1 d.c. into each of next 18 (24:30) d.c., 2 d.c. into next d.c., 1 d.c. into each of next 34 d.c., 1 ch., turn. 90 (96:102) d.c.

5th row: 1 d.c. into each d.c. to end, 1 ch., turn.

6th row: 1 d.c. into each of next 34 d.c., 2 d.c. into next d.c., 1 d.c. into each of next 20 (26:32) d.c., 2 d.c. into next d.c., 1 d.c. into each of next 34 d.c.

7th to 16th rows: Work 10 rows in d.c., increasing 2 sts. on the 8th, 10th, 12th, 14th and 16th of these rows, working 34 d.c. at each end of rows and 2 sts. more between increases on each successive inc. row. 102 (108:114) d.c.

17th to 20th rows: Work 4 rows straight. **

Continue to shape dart.

21st row: 1 d.c. into each d.c. until 35 d.c. remain unworked, turn.

22nd row: S.s. into 1st d.c., 1 d.c. into each d.c. until 35 d.c. remain unworked, turn.

23rd and 24th rows: S.s. into 1st d.c., 1 d.c. into each d.c. and s.s. until 28 d.c. remain on each row, turn.

25th and 26th rows: S.s. into 1st d.c., 1 d.c. into each d.c. and s.s. until 21 d.c. remain on each row, turn.

27th to 32nd rows: As last 2 rows but work 7 sts. more on each row, on 32nd row all sts. will have been worked.

33rd to 36th rows: Work 4 rows straight, omitting 1 ch. at end of last row.

To shape armholes

1st row: S.s. over 4 (5:6) d.c., 1 d.c., into each d.c. until 4 (5:6) d.c. remain, turn.

2nd row: S.s. over 3 d.c., 1 d.c. into each d.c. until 3 d.c. remain, turn. 88 (92:96) d.c.

To shape neck and continue armhole shaping

Next row: S.s. over 2 d.c., 1 ch., 1 d.c. into each of next 26 d.c., 1 ch., turn and work on these 27 d.c.

First shoulder

1st row: * Insert hook into next d.c., draw through loop; repeat from * once, yarn over hook and draw through 3 loops on hook – 1 d.c. decreased, 1 d.c. into each d.c. until 2 d.c. remain, turn.

2nd row: S.s. over 2 d.c., 1 d.c. into each d.c. until 3 d.c. remain, dec. 1 d.c., 1 d.c. into turning ch., 1 ch., turn.

3rd row: As 1st row. 18 d.c.

4th to 7th rows: Dec. 1 st. at armhole edge, as given for neck decreases, on each row. 14 d.c.

8th row: Straight in d.c.

9th row: Dec. 1 st. at armhole edge.

10th and 11th rows: As 8th and 9th rows. 12 d.c. Work 6 rows straight.

Continue to shape for arm and neck edges

1st row: Inc. 1 st. at armhole edge and dec. 1 st. at neck edge.

2nd to 11th rows: Straight in d.c. Repeat last 11 rows and 1st row again. 12 d.c. Continue straight in d.c. until work measures 6½ (7:7½) in. from beginning of armhole shaping, ending at armhole edge.

To slope shoulder

1st row: S.s. over 4 d.c., 1 d.c. into each d.c. to end, 1 ch., turn.

2nd row: 1 d.c. into each of next 3 d.c., s.s. into next d.c. and fasten off. Miss centre 30 (34:38) d.c., join yarn to next d.c.

Second shoulder

1st row: 1 ch., 1 d.c. into each of next 26 d.c., turn. 27 d.c. Now complete to match 1st shoulder.

BACK BODICE

Work as for front bodice until ** is reached. Continue straight in d.c. until work measures same as front from ch. edge to armhole.

To shape armholes

1st and 2nd rows: As 1st and 2nd rows of armhole shaping on front.

3rd to 6th rows: S.s. over 2 d.c., 1 d.c. into each d.c. until 2 d.c. remain, turn.

7th to 10th rows: Dec. 1 st., as before, at both ends of each row.

continued

11th to 14th rows: Dec. 1 st. at beginning of each row. 60 (64:68) d.c. Work 6 rows straight. Inc. 1 st. at both ends of the next and following 11th row. Work 3 rows straight. 64 (68:72) d.c.

To shape neck
First shoulder
1st row: 1 d.c. into each of next 14 d.c., 1 ch., turn and work on these 15 d.c.
2nd to 4th rows: Dec. 1 st. at neck edge on each row. 12 d.c.
5th to 7th rows: Straight in d.c.
8th row: Dec. 1 st. at neck edge and inc. 1 st. at armhole edge. Continue straight in d.c. until armhole measures same as front, ending at armhole edge. Slope shoulder as given for front. Miss centre 34 (38:42) d.c., rejoin yarn to next st., 1 ch., 1 d.c. into each of next 14 d.c., 1 ch., turn and work on 15 d.c.

Second shoulder
Complete to match 1st shoulder. Very lightly press bodice on the wrong side with a cool iron over a dry cloth. Join right side seam only.

SKIRT
Worked in one piece
With right side of bodice facing, using No. 10 hook, join yarn to back bodice at left side opening.
1st foundation row: 1 ch., then working through foundation ch., and decreasing 3 sts. to avoid 'holes', work 84 (90:96) d.c. along back bodice, decreasing 4 sts., work 84 (90:96) d.c. along front bodice, turn. 169 (181:193) d.c.
2nd foundation row: 3 ch. to stand for 1st tr., miss 3 d.c., * into next d.c. work 2 tr., 1 ch., 2 tr. – 1 group worked, 1 ch., miss 5 d.c.; repeat from * ending miss 2 d.c., 1 tr. into last d.c., turn. 28 (30:32) groups. Now work in pattern as follows.
1st row: 1 ch., * into 1 ch. sp. of group on previous row work 1 group, 1 ch.; repeat from * ending 1 d.c. into 3rd of 3 ch., turn.
2nd row: 3 ch., * 1 group into 1 ch. sp. of group, 3 ch., then insert hook under 1 ch. between groups and 2 rows down and work 1 d.c. thus forming a scallop, 3 ch.; repeat from * ending 1 group into 1 ch. sp., 1 tr. into d.c., turn.
3rd row: 3 ch., * 1 group into 1 ch. sp., 1 ch.; repeat from * ending 1 tr. into 3rd of 3 ch., turn. Break off Crysette or Stalite, join in Goldfingering.
4th row: Using No. 9 hook and Goldfingering work as for 1st row. Break off Goldfingering join in Crysette or Stalite. Change to No. 10 hook.

5th row: As 2nd row.
6th row: As 3rd row.
7th to 11th rows: As 1st to 5th rows.
12th row: 3 ch., * into 1 ch. sp. of group work 3 tr., 1 ch., 3 tr. – increased group worked, 1 ch.; repeat from * ending 1 tr. into 3rd of 3 ch. Continue in pattern with increased groups as set, and work 11 rows straight, do not turn after 11th row, 8 complete rows of scallops have been formed and right side of work is facing. Close side opening and continue to work in rounds as follows.

1st round: S.s. over to 1st ch. sp. in group, 3 ch.; 3 tr., 1 ch., 4 tr. into same sp. – increased group worked, 1 ch.; * 4 tr., 1 ch., 4 tr. into next 1 ch. sp., 1 ch.; repeat from * to end, s.s. to 3rd of 3 ch. to join.
2nd round: As 1st round.
3rd round: S.s. to 1st ch. sp. in group, 3 ch., 1 group into same sp., * 3 ch., then insert hook under 1 ch. between groups and 2 rows down and work 1 d.c., 3 ch., 1 group into 1 ch. sp. between groups; repeat from * ending s.s. into 3rd of 3 ch. Continue in pattern and rounds with increased groups, as set, working every 6th round in Goldfingering and No. 9 hook, until dress measures 44½ (45:45½) in. when hanging, or 8 in. less than finished length required, ending with completion of scallop which contains a row of Goldfingering. Place a marker on last round.

Back vent opening Optional
Fold work in half along centre back, so that fold comes between groups. Mark fold on last scallop worked to indicate position of vent opening. Fasten off yarn. With right side of work facing, rejoin yarn to last tr. worked on group before marker.
Next row: 3 ch., turn so that wrong side of work is facing, then work in pattern to marker, turn. Continue working in rows until work measures 8 in. from beginning of vent opening, ending with a 2nd pattern row. Fasten off.
If vent is omitted continue in rounds for a further 8 in. from marked round, ending with a 2nd pattern round, then fasten off.

NECK EDGING
First join shoulder seams. Using No. 10 hook and Crysette or Stalite, with right side facing and beginning at one shoulder seam, work 2 rounds of d.c. evenly around neck edge, then using Goldfingering work 1 round of d.c. over d.c.; fasten off and sew in all ends.

ARMHOLE EDGINGS
Right armhole
Beginning at underarm seam, work as for neck edging.

Left armhole
Work as for neck edging but work in rows.

RIBBON
Using Goldfingering and No. 9 hook make 4 ch.
1st row: 1 d.c. into 2nd ch. from hook, 1 d.c. into each of 2 ch., 1 ch., turn.
2nd row: 1 d.c. into each d.c. to end, 1 ch., turn.
Repeat the last row until ribbon is long enough, when slightly stretched, to go round bodice and skirt join, plus 6 in. for bow; then fasten off.

MAKING UP
Very lightly press dress and ribbon on the wrong side with a cool iron over a dry cloth. With right side of dress facing, using Crysette or Stalite and No. 10 hook, work 1 row of d.c. along row ends of opening at left side, also along row ends of vent, if worked, to neaten. With slide on zip ¼ in. from underarm, neatly sew in zip fastener. Sew hook and eye to top. Place one end of ribbon to centre front and centrally over bodice and skirt join, pin ribbon around dress, leaving 6 in. free, then very neatly s.s. ribbon into position. With remaining ribbon, make a flat imitation bow, s.s. under edge of bow to dress.

SKIRT LINING
First take the following measurements from dress: Length from bodice join to 1st increased group, from 1st increased group to 2nd, then from 2nd to hem edge; width across skirt at each increased group, top and hem edge. Take a long sheet of paper and use one long side as centre front or centre back. Mark out total length, halve width measurements and mark, then draw in side seam. Allowing ½ in. at top, 2 in. at hem and 1 in. at side seam, cut out pattern. Waist darts: At top edge mark 3½ in. in from centre, 10 in. below mark 3½ in. in from centre and draw a line to connect marks. Fold material in half lengthwise, place pattern with centre to fold and cut out, tailor tack side seam and dart line. Remove pattern and cut a second piece. Darts: On the wrong side of each piece, tack darts taking ½ in. at top and tapering to point at end. Omitting 1 in. seams measure top edge of lining to ascertain correct measurement, if necessary adjust darts. Stitch

darts and press towards centre. Leaving left side open for approximately 10 in. tack and machine side seams. Press seams open. Neaten all seams and top edge. At lower edge turn under ½ in. and machine. If vent has been worked cut up centre back for approximately 10 in. and make a very narrow hem. Turn up a further 2 in. hem and s.s. into position and press – edge of lining should be level with 'V' at scalloped edge. With right side of lining to wrong side of dress, opening at left, very neatly herringbone lining to bodice and skirt join. S.s. lining over zip tapes. If desired lining can be s.s. to vent opening.

BOLERO
Front
Using No. 10 hook and Crysette or Stalite, commence with 110 (116: 122) ch. Work the 1st and 2nd rows as given for front bodice on dress.

To shape armholes
1st and 2nd rows: As 1st and 2nd rows of armhole shaping on front bodice of dress. 96 (100: 104) d.c.
3rd to 10th rows: Dec. 1 st., as given on dress, at both ends of every row. 80 (84: 88) d.c. Continue straight until work measures 5 in. from beginning of armhole shaping.

To shape neck
First shoulder
1st row: 1 d.c. into each of next 33 (34: 35) d.c., 1 ch., turn and work on these 34 (35: 36) d.c.
2nd to 8th rows: Dec. 1 st. at neck edge on each row. 27 (28: 29) d.c. Continue straight until work measures 6½ (7: 7½) in. from beginning of armhole shaping, ending at armhole edge.

To slope shoulder
1st row: S.s. over 4 d.c., 1 d.c. into each d.c. to end, 1 ch., turn.
2nd row: 1 d.c. into each d.c. until 4 d.c. remain, turn. Repeat last 2 rows twice. Fasten off. Miss centre 12 (14: 16) d.c., rejoin yarn to next st., 1 ch., 1 d.c. into each d.c. to end, 1 ch., turn and work on these 34 (35: 36) d.c.

Second shoulder
Complete to match 1st shoulder.

Right or left half back
(*both alike as work is reversible*)
Using No. 10 hook commence with 54 (57: 60) ch. Work 1st and 2nd rows as on front.

To shape armhole
1st row: S.s. over 4 (5: 6) d.c., 1 ch., 1 d.c. into each d.c. to end, 1 ch., turn.
2nd row: 1 d.c. into each d.c. until 3 d.c. remain, 1 ch., turn.
3rd to 10th rows: Dec. 1 st. at armhole edge on each row. 39 (41: 43) d.c. Continue straight until armhole measures same as back, ending at armhole edge.

To slope shoulder and shape neck
1st row: S.s. over 4 d.c., 1 ch., 1 d.c. into each d.c. to end, 1 ch., turn.
2nd row: 1 d.c. into each d.c. until 4 d.c. remain, turn.
3rd row: S.s. over 4 d.c., 1 ch., 1 d.c. into each d.c. until 9 (10: 11) d.c. remain, 1 ch., turn.
4th row: Dec. 1 st., 1 d.c. into each d.c. until 4 d.c. remain, turn.
5th row: S.s. over 4 d.c., 1 ch., 1 d.c. into each d.c. until 3 d.c. remain, dec., 1 d.c., 1 ch., turn.
6th row: As 4th row. Fasten off.

SLEEVES (*both alike*)
Using No. 10 hook commence with 68 (74: 80) ch. Work the 1st and 2nd rows as on front.

To shape top
Work the 1st and 2nd rows of armhole shaping on front bodice on dress. Dec. 1 st. at beginning of every row until 28 (29: 30) d.c. remain. Dec. 1 st. at both ends of every row until 16 (17: 18) d.c. remain.
Next row: S.s. over 2 d.c., 1 ch., 1 d.c. into each d.c. until 2 d.c. remain, 1 ch., turn. 12 (13: 14) d.c. Work 1 row, then fasten off.

LOWER EDGINGS
First join the 2 straight row ends to form part of side seam. With wrong side facing, using No. 10 hook and Crysette or Stalite, join yarn to ch. edge at left half back, working through base of sts. on 1st row and decreasing 1 st. at each side seam, 1 st. on each half back and 2 sts. on front, to avoid 'holes', work 211 (223: 235) d.c. evenly along bolero.
1st row: As 2nd foundation row on skirt. 35 (37: 39) groups.
2nd row: As 4th pattern row on skirt.
3rd row: As 5th pattern row on skirt.
4th row: 5 ch., * 1 d.c. into 1 ch. sp. in group, 5 ch.; repeat from * ending 1 d.c. into 1 ch. sp. in last group, 2 ch., 1 tr. into 3rd ch., 1 ch., turn.
5th row: 1 d.c. into 1st tr., 2 d.c. into 2 ch. sp.,

* 1 d.c. into d.c. in group, 5 d.c. into 5 ch. sp.; repeat from * ending 1 d.c. into next d.c. in group, 3 d.c. into last sp., 1 ch., turn. 211 (223: 235) d.c.
6th to 8th rows: 1 d.c. into each d.c. to end, 1 ch., turn.
9th to 11th rows: As 1st to 3rd rows. Fasten off.

SLEEVE EDGINGS (*both alike*)
With wrong side facing using No. 10 hook and Crysette or Stalite, join yarn to 1st st. and work 67 (73: 79) d.c. along sleeve edge. Now work from the 1st to 11th row as given for lower edging.

MAKING UP
Press as for dress. Join shoulder seams. Join sleeve seams. Set in sleeves.

EDGING
With right side of work facing using No. 10 hook and Crysette or Stalite, join yarn to lower edge of left half back and work 1 row of d.c. evenly along row ends of back, around neck edge and down right half back, fasten off. Using Goldfingering work 1 row of d.c. over d.c. along neck edge only and fasten off.

TO COMPLETE
Make a button loop at neck edge on left half back and sew button to right half back to correspond.

See page 94 for washing instructions.
Do not use enzyme washing powders that remove stains.

A lacy summer jumper

continued from page 66

Shape neck
** 1st row: One 2 ch. sp. in centre of first 5 tr. blk., 1 ch., 1 d.c. in first single tr., * 1 ch., one 2 ch. sp. in centre of next 5 tr. blk., 1 ch., 1 d.c. in next single tr., rep. from * once, 3 ch., turn.
2nd row: 5 tr. in first 2 ch. sp., patt. to end, 3 ch., turn. **
3rd row: Patt. to end, 3 ch., turn.
4th row: Patt. to end.

Shape shoulder
Sl.st. over first 6 (6; 6; 9) tr., patt. to end. Fasten

off. Miss the centre 4 (5; 6; 7) 5 tr. blks., rejoin yarn to next single tr. and complete to correspond with first side.

BACK

Work exactly as given for Front until work measures 2 rows more than Front to comm. of shoulder shaping, then work from ** to ** as given for Front.

Shape shoulder as given for Front. Miss the centre 4 (5; 6; 7) 5 tr. blks., rejoin yarn to next tr. and work to correspond with other side.

SLEEVES

Using No. 8 hook make 49 (49; 55; 55) ch. and work the first row as given for Front. 8 (8; 9; 9) 5 tr. blks. Work 2 rows in patt.

Using No. 7 hook proceed as follows:

4th row: 1 d.c. on first tr. (inc. made), one 2 ch. sp. on first 5 tr. blk., patt. to last tr. (3 ch. of previous row), 1 ch., 2 d.c. in top ch. of 3 ch. of previous row (inc. made), 3 ch., turn, to count as first tr. on next row.

5th row: Miss first d.c., 1 tr. in next d.c., 5 tr. blk. in next 2 ch. sp., patt. to last 2 d.c., 1 tr. in each d.c., 3 ch., turn, to count as first d.c. on next row.

6th row: Miss first tr., 1 d.c. on next tr., 1 ch., patt. to last 2 tr., 1 ch., 1 d.c. on each tr., 3 ch., turn.

7th row: 1 tr. on each of first 2 d.c. (inc. made), patt. to last 2 d.c., 1 tr. on each d.c., 1 tr. into same place as last d.c. (inc. made), 3 ch., turn.

8th row: Miss first tr., 1 d.c. in next tr., 1 ch., 1 d.c. in next tr., patt. to last 3 tr., work 1 d.c. into first tr., 1 ch., 1 d.c. in each of next 2 tr., 3 ch., turn.

9th row: 2 tr. in first d.c., patt. to last d.c., 3 tr. in end d.c., 3 ch., turn.

10th row: One 2 ch. sp. in centre of 3 tr., 1 ch., patt. to last 3 tr., one 2 ch. sp. in centre of 3 tr., 1 ch., 1 d.c., in end tr., 3 ch., turn.

11th row: 5 tr. in centre of first 2 ch. sp., patt. to last 2 ch. sp., work 5 tr. in this sp., 1 tr. in top ch. of 3 ch. of previous row. 10 (10; 11; 11) 5 tr. blks. Fasten off.

Break yarn, turn work.

Shape top

Rejoin yarn to centre of second 5 tr. blk., one

2 ch. sp. in centre of blk., patt. to last 5 tr. blk., turn.

1st row: 3 tr. in first 2 ch. sp., patt. to end, working 3 tr. in end 2 ch. sp., turn.

2nd row: 1 d.c. in centre of first 3 tr., 1 ch., patt. to last 3 tr., 1 ch., 1 d.c. in centre of 3 tr., 2 ch., turn.

3rd row: 5 tr. in first 2 ch. sp., 1 tr. in next d.c., patt. to last 2 ch. sp., 5 tr. in this sp., 1 d.c. on end d.c., turn.

4th row: 1 ch., one 2 ch. sp. in centre of next 5 tr. blk., patt. to end, working 1 ch., 1 d.c. on top ch. of previous row.

5th row: 3 tr. in first 2 ch. sp., patt. to end, working 3 tr. in end sp., turn.

6th row: One 2 ch. sp. in centre of 3 tr. blk., patt. to last 3 tr. blk., one 2 ch. sp. on this blk., 3 ch., turn.

7th row: As 1st. **8th row:** As 2nd.

9th row: As 3rd.

Fasten off.

TO MAKE UP

Using a damp cloth and a warm iron press carefully. Sew up shoulder seams. Sew in sleeves. Sew up side and sleeve seams.

Neck border

Using No. 11 crochet hook, rejoin yarn to left shoulder and work as follows:

Work 10 d.c. down to corner of neck, work 2 d.c. into corner, 28 d.c. across centre Front, 2 d.c. into corner, 10 d.c. up right side of neck, 5 d.c. down right back neck, 28 d.c. across Back neck, and 5 d.c. up left back neck.

Next round: * Miss 2 d.c., 2 d.c., 3 ch., 2 d.c. in next d.c., rep. from * to first corner, work 2 d.c. into corner, cont. in this manner all around neck. Fasten off.

Border pattern: With right side facing, rejoin yarn to sleeve seam, work 2 d.c., 3 ch., 2 d.c. into centre of first 5 tr. blk., 2 d.c., 3 ch., 2 d.c. into first single tr., * 2 d.c., 3 ch., 2 d.c. into centre of next 5 tr. blk., 2 d.c., 3 ch., 2 d.c. into next single tr., rep. from * all around sleeve. Fasten off. Work the other sleeve edge in same manner then rejoin yarn to side seam of lower edge of sweater and rep. the border pattern all around.

Fasten off. Press all seams.

Tingha and Tucker – two famous bears *Illustrated on page 32*

Materials:
TINGHA
3 2-oz balls Lister Fun-Fur-Knit, Beige.

TUCKER
2 2-oz balls Lister Fun-Fur-Knit, Beige.
1 2-oz ball Lister Fun-Fur-Knit, White.

For each Bear:
1 pair bear eyes with safety clips.
1 nose with safety clip.
Small quantity black double knitting wool for
claws.
½ yd (45·7 cm) 36 in. (91·4 cm) wide material for
lining. Small, washable foam chippings, for
stuffing.
¾ yd (68·6 cm) 1 in. (2·5 cm) wide gold ribbon
for bow tie.
Crochet hook Nos. 2 (7·00 mm).
                   9 (3·50 mm) for claws.

Measurements: Height 10 in.; ear span 9½ in.

Tension:
5 double crochet stitches = 3 in. (approx.)
4 rows = 2½ in. (approx.)

Abbreviations:

ch. chain	st. stitch
d.c. double crochet	sl.st. slip stitch

Joining Fun-Fur-Knit: Strip pile away from
binding threads for 3 in. on the two pieces to
be joined. Take binding threads on both ends
and tie in a secure knot, ensuring that the
remaining tufts are drawn together, leaving no
gap before completing the knot. Check that the
knot does not slip before trimming the binding
threads.

Note: *Draw up all chain stitches and loops in*
double crochet to a good ½ in. to allow full free-
dom for pile.

BASE
Using No. 2 crochet hook, make 8 ch. (very
loosely).
1st row: 1 d.c. into 2nd ch. from hook, 6 d.c.,
1 ch., turn. **2nd row:** 7 d.c. **3rd row:** 7 d.c. **4th**
row: 1 sl.st., 5 d.c., turn. **5th row:** 1 sl.st., 3 d.c.
Fasten off.

BACK
Using No. 2 crochet hook make 20 ch.
1st row: 1 d.c. in 2nd ch. from hook, 18 d.c.,

1 ch., turn. **2nd row:** 19 d.c., 1 ch., turn. **3rd**
row: 19 d.c., turn. **4th row:** 3 sl.st., 13 d.c., 1 ch.,
turn. Now increase for front paws. **5th row:**
2 d.c. in first st., 11 d.c., 2 d.c. in next st., turn.
6th row: 2 d.c. in first st., 13 d.c., 2 d.c. in last
st., 1 ch., turn. **7th row:** 17 d.c., 1 ch., turn. **8th**
row: 17 d.c., 1 ch., turn. **9th row:** 17 d.c., turn.
10th row: 4 sl.st., 9 d.c., 1 ch., turn. **11th row:**
Now increase for ears. 2 d.c. in first st., 7 d.c.,
2 d.c. in last st., 1 ch., turn. **12th row:** 2 d.c. in
first st., 9 d.c., 2 d.c. in last st., 1 ch., turn. **13th**
row: 2 d.c. in first st., 11 d.c., 2 d.c. in last st.,
1 ch., turn. **14th row:** 2 d.c. in first st., 13 d.c.,
2 d.c. in last st., 1 ch., turn. **15th row:** 2 d.c. in
first st., 1 d.c., 2 d.c. in next st., sl.st. to last
3 sts., 2 d.c. in next st., 1 d.c., 2 d.c. in last st.
16th row: 5 d.c., sl.st. to last 5 sts., 5 d.c. Fasten
off.

FRONT
This is worked in beige for *Tingha* and in white
for *Tucker.*
Using No. 2 hook make 13 ch.
1st row: 1 d.c. in 2nd ch. from hook, 11 d.c.,
1 ch., turn. **2nd row:** 12 d.c., 1 ch., turn. **3rd**
row: 12 d.c., turn. **4th row:** 2 sl.st., 8 d.c., turn
with 1 ch. **5th row:** 2 d.c. in first st., 6 d.c., 2 d.c.
in last st. **6th row:** 2 d.c. in first st., 8 d.c., 2 d.c.
in last st. **7th row:** 12 d.c., 1 ch., turn. **8th row:**
12 d.c., turn. **9th row:** 2 sl.st., 8 d.c., turn. **10th**
row: 1 sl.st., 6 d.c. Fasten off.

FACE
Using No. 2 hook make 2 ch. in beige yarn.
1st round: Join with sl.st. into a ring and work
6 d.c. into it.
Note: Mark the first st. of every round with
small safety pin, moving it up each time.
2nd round: 2 d.c. into each d.c. of previous
round (12 d.c.). **3rd round:** 2 d.c. in first st.,
5 d.c. in next 5 sts., 2 d.c. in next st., d.c. to end
of round (14 d.c.). **4th round:** (2 d.c. in 1st st.,
1 d.c. in next st.) repeat to end of round (21
d.c.). **5th round:** 2 d.c. in 1st st., 4 d.c. in next
4 sts., 2 d.c. in next st., 4 d.c. in next 4 sts., 2 d.c.
in next st., 4 d.c. in next 4 sts., 2 d.c. in next st.,
5 d.c.

THE EARS
For *Tingha* continue in beige yarn.
For *Tucker* break off beige and join white.
Starting at end of last round
First ear: **1st row:** 1 ch., 5 d.c., 1 ch., turn. **2nd**

row: 5 d.c., turn. **3rd row:** 5 d.c., turn. **4th row:** 1 sl.st., 3 d.c., turn. **5th row:** 3 sl.st. Fasteh off yarn.

Second ear: With right side of work facing, miss 12 sts. at forehead. Rejoin yarn. **1st row:** 5 d.c., 1 ch., turn. **2nd row:** 5 d.c., turn. **3rd row:** 5 d.c., turn. **4th row:** 1 sl.st., 3 d.c., turn. **5th row:** 3 sl.st. Fasten off yarn.

CLAWS
Using No. 9 hook with black yarn, make 6 ch. **1st row:** 1 d.c. in 2nd ch. from hook, 4 d.c., turn. **2nd row:** 5 d.c., 1 ch., turn. **3rd row:** 5 d.c., turn. **4th row:** (5 ch., 1 sl.st. into 4th ch. from hook for picot, 1 d.c.) 4 times (5 picots). Fasten off yarn. Work 3 more claws similarly.

TO MAKE UP
Lining: Leaving sufficient lining material for the face, lay the crocheted back, front and base on the fabric, allowing ½ in. turnings all round. Cut out.

Pin centre of remaining piece of lining into nose section of the face, folding excess material across the face. Cut all round, allowing ½ in. for turnings.

Turn in lining and tack to crochet pieces all round edges, with several tacking stitches across each piece.
Be sure to remove all pins as you go.

Test-stuff the nose and mark position of eyes and nose with a pin. Remove test stuffing, clip eyes and nose into place.

Note: If preferred, the eyes and nose can be made from pieces of felt ¼ in. diameter in dark brown for pupils, placed over gold or yellow ½ in. diameter, buttonhole stitched into position. The nose can be a piece of black felt, or simply embroidered in black yarn.

On the wrong side, stitching firmly with double cotton, catching lining and fur with every stitch, join head, ear, face and neck seams.

Place one claw, with picots showing, in position at the extremity of each front paw and stitch.

Turn bear to the right side and stuff so far.

Join side seams and back legs by over-sewing, again inserting two claws, and stuff.

Join long straight side of base to front of bear and stitch. Finish stuffing and join lower leg seams and the remaining base seam, making sure stuffing is evenly distributed and bear will sit up.

Tie ribbon in a neat bow and catch stitch at shoulders and through first tie of bow.

WASHING
Hand wash in warm water. Do not rub. Follow with a cold rinse. Do not wring.

Suit *continued from page 68*

To make up
Pin out and press each piece on wrong side under a damp cloth. Join shoulder, side and sleeve seams. Set in sleeves, placing centre of head of sleeve to shoulder seam. Sew cuffs neatly in position. Sew pocket flaps neatly in position. Sew on buttons to correspond with button-holes. Sew buttons on pocket flaps. Fold neckband in half on to wrong side and sew neatly in position. Press all seams.

SKIRT *(back and front alike)*
For 38 in. hip follow figures in parenthesis ( ). For 40 in. hip follow figures in brackets [ ].

Using No. 8 crochet hook, ch. 94 (100) [106] and work in pattern as Back until work measures 3 (3) [3] in. Now decrease 1 st. at each end of next and every following 8th row

until 84 (90) [92] sts. remain. Continue on these sts. until work measures 15½ (15½) [15½] in. from commencement (adjust length here).
Next row: Pattern 14, * hook into next st., pull yarn through leaving 2 loops on hook, work next st., yarn through all 3 loops on hook (1 st. decreased), rep. from * once more, pattern to last 18 sts., rep. from * to * twice, pattern to end.
Work 5 rows straight. Rep. last 6 rows twice more.
Continue in pattern until work measures 21 (21) [21] in, or required length. Fasten off.

To make up
Pin out and press each piece on wrong side under a damp cloth. Join side seams. Join elastic into circle and make herringbone st. casing over elastic at waist. Press seams.

Finishing, laundering and general care

The final stages are of paramount importance in the finishing of crochet work. Many well-made articles lose the professional look for four main reasons:

1. Incorrect, inadequate or lack of pinning out to correct measurements.
2. Over-pressing or no pressing at all.
3. Carelessness in sewing up.
4. Haphazard laundering.

It does seem incredible that some people will take the utmost pains with the actual crochet, yet are prepared to leave the final stages to chance. The old adage, 'If a job is worth doing, it is worth doing well', applies to crochet at every stage of the work.

Much crochet work of yesterday, made by our forbears, still graces some homes as treasured heirlooms. With proper care, there is no reason why today's crocheted gems should not take their place in the households of future generations.

Crochet in the home is meant to be used. It is very hard-wearing, but without proper after-care, discolouration will almost surely result. It should never be left unused and forgotten in the seclusion of drawer or linen cupboard.

One general rule must always be followed. That is, to carry out carefully the advice given with the pattern and with the yarn.

Pinning out, or blocking

All finished work, sections of garments, etc., should be placed right side down on the ironing board or table, and pinned out to the correct measurements. Geometric shapes, picots, flower petals and loops should be pinned carefully to their correct shapes.

Pressing

Pressing can enhance or ruin crochet work. For every kind of crochet, pressure means *press and lift the iron* – it must never be pushed along as in ordinary ironing.

The iron should be warm, never hot, except in the case of starched cottons.

Never press raised patterns. If the iron is held about ½ in. above the work for a few seconds it will provide the necessary amount of steam to set the work into the correct shape.

Press each seam after sewing up – never wait until all the seams are sewn. Instruction leaflets usually give the order of sewing up.

Always allow the fabric time to cool before removing the pins.

The general rule when using a pressing cloth is :
Damp for woollens, cottons and pure silks,
Dry for synthetic yarns.

Seams A short, blunt-ended wool needle should be used for sewing the seams of woollen and similar synthetic materials, and finer pointed needles for cottons.

When two identical seams have to be made, both should be sewn in the same direction.

Several types of seam may be used for joining crochet work according to the pattern of the fabric to be joined.

Motif joining is described on page 48.

Crocheted seam
This is suitable for plain fabric. Place the right sides of the material facing each other, and work along the wrong side.

Work a single row of double crochet stitches, taking up one stitch from each side of work. These stitches should be neat and even, and sufficiently loose to avoid puckering, yet of a reasonable tightness to obviate any sagging.

Flat seam (A)   Back-stitch seam   Crocheted seam

Back-stitch seam

This seam is both strong and reasonably invisible.

Place the work with right sides facing each other, and join in the sewing yarn.

Working one stitch inside the edge of the fabric, bring the needle through from the back of the work, then replace it slightly beyond where it came through, return it the same distance away. Put back the needle each time into the end of the last stitch. This gives a machine-stitching effect.

Flat seam (A)

A flat seam should always be used for infants' garments to prevent chafing.

Place right sides of both pieces together. Join yarn through from the back. With the first finger of left hand between both pieces, and using a very small stitch just inside the edges, take needle through to back of work. Again taking a very small stitch, return needle to front again.

Flat seam (B)

This method is specially suitable for openwork patterns when some slight weaving is necessary to avoid unsightly holes appearing.

Lay both pieces side by side, right sides downwards. Join in the sewing yarn. Take needle through one edge stitch, then through the corresponding one on the other piece, and pull gently together, tightly enough to secure without puckering.

If openings appear in the sides, these should be neatly woven over and into the seam.

Shoulder seam

Shoulder seams
These should be carefully pinned together, and sewn with a fine back-stitch seam. Any shaping steps should be sewn diagonally across.

Inserting the sleeve When setting in sleeves, first pin the centre top of sleeve to the shoulder seam. Then pin underarm seams, and working alternately at each side, pin the sleeve edges to the armhole edges, easing in any fullness, and matching patterns. A fine back-stitch seam gives the best finish.

Collars These should be carefully pinned to the main work, centre to centre and secured with a back-stitch seam.

Pockets Tack carefully into position and slip stitch invisibly.

Skirt waist *Elastic*
Cut elastic to size and join ends together. Pin to skirt waist and secure with herringbone stitches made just below and above the elastic.

Petersham
For a more tailored look, shaped petersham with fastening attached is simple and quick to fix and neat in appearance. Panda-PAK make this in various lengths and widths.

Lining There is no necessity to line crocheted garments. A plain, tailored slip is sufficient to stop seating in skirts, and to give the necessary cover-up under openwork crochet.

Fastenings Zip fasteners are available in many colours and are frequently graded to suit various kinds of garment.
Velcro is an easily-fixed touch-and-close fastening material which gives a firm, neat and washable closure.

Joining crochet to material Place crochet in position on material, and pin securely. Mark the outline of the crochet by a row of tacking stitches. Remove crochet and turn under a narrow hem on material, with the tacking stitches on the outside fold. Slip stitch the hem, then overcast the crochet to fold.

The method used to join edgings to materials is given on page 40.

Laundering   Washing instructions given with the recommended yarn should always be followed, but general washing instructions are given below.

Most yarns are now colour-fast, with shrink-resistant finishes, but great care in washing is essential.

If in doubt about colour-fastness, a tablespoonful of salt added to both washing and rinsing water will usually fix the colour.

Wash in warm, *never* hot water. Pure soap flakes or powders give good results, and most other powders are quite satisfactory. They should be completely dissolved before the article is immersed. Squeeze the lather gently through the material – *never* rub or wring. Crocheted articles should never be allowed to become so bady soiled as to make rubbing necessary.

Several changes of rinsing water should be used to remove all traces of soap or detergent. The temperature should be constant.

Squeeze out surplus water and roll the article loosely in a towel. Dry flat where possible. Never leave sleeves to dangle; fold over the ends to avoid stretching.

Cottons   The above instructions apply equally to cottons, but when starching is necessary, washing should be followed by dabbing on or spraying on a solution of starch. It should be applied to the article after pinning out. Light pressing may follow with a hot iron.

To make a starch solution: 1 teaspoonful of starch powder to ½-pint of water gives a good consistency.

Dry-cleaning   Dry cleaners today are fully conversant with the special demands of all natural and synthetic fibres. It is advisable, however, to tell the cleaner the type of material he is to clean, and the cause of any particular stain, in case special treatment is required.

After-care   Crocheted garments, particularly dresses and skirts, should never be left suspended for long periods on a wardrobe hanger. They are all reasonably crease-resistant, and storage in a roomy drawer is less likely to lead to drooping shoulders and dropping hemlines.

Index